Visitor's G  **W9-BLT-830**
Malta & Gozo

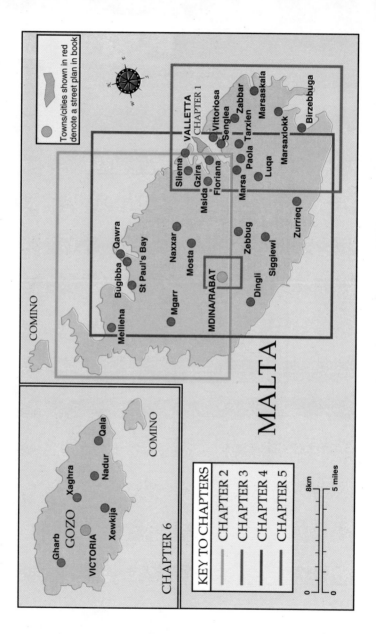

VISITOR'S GUIDE

MALTA
& GOZO

GEOFFREY BROWN

MPC
HUNTER
PUBLISHING INC

Published by:
Moorland Publishing Co Ltd,
Moor Farm Road West,
Ashbourne,
Derbyshire DE6 1HD
England

ISBN 0 86190 308 0

Published in the USA by:
Hunter Publishing Inc,
300 Raritan Center Parkway,
CN 94, Edison, NJ 08818

ISBN 1 55650 595 7 (USA)

British Library Cataloguing in
Publication Data:
A catalogue record for this book is
available from the British Library.

Colour origination by:
P. & W. Graphics Pte Ltd, Singapore

Printed by Wing King Tong Co Ltd

Front cover photograph:
St Julian's Bay *(Maltese Tourist
Office)*
Rear cover photograph: Festa,
Malta *(Author)*

Illustrations have been supplied as
follows: Pages 10, 11, 74, 142,
Maltese Tourist Office; pages 51,
66, W Clarke. All other illustrations
supplied by the author.

MPC Production Team:
Editorial: Tonya Monk
Design: Dan Clarke
Cartography: Alastair Morrison
Typesetting: Christine Haines

Acknowledgements
Many thanks are due to Connie
Grech of the Maltese Tourist Office
in Valletta, and to Mario Falzon, an
excellent guide and an invaluable
font of knowledge. Any mistakes
in this text are my responsibility,
not his. Thanks also to Spot for his
technical assistance.

Dedication: For Jo, this one too.

CONTENTS

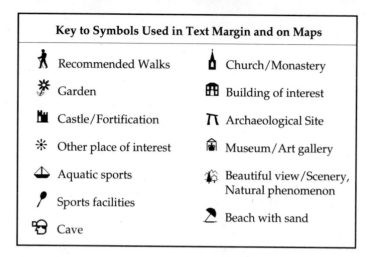

Key to Symbols Used in Text Margin and on Maps

🚶 Recommended Walks

🌺 Garden

🏰 Castle/Fortification

✳ Other place of interest

⛵ Aquatic sports

🎾 Sports facilities

🐚 Cave

⛪ Church/Monastery

🏛 Building of interest

Π Archaeological Site

🏛 Museum/Art gallery

🍃 Beautiful view/Scenery, Natural phenomenon

⌐ Beach with sand

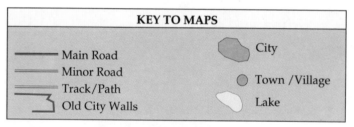

KEY TO MAPS

——— Main Road

——— Minor Road

——— Track/Path

⌐ Old City Walls

City

Town /Village

Lake

How To Use This Guide

This MPC Visitor's Guide has been designed to be as easy to use as possible. Each chapter covers a region or itinerary in a natural progression which gives all the background information to help you enjoy your visit. MPC's distinctive margin symbols, the important places printed in bold, and a comprehensive index enable the reader to find the most interesting places to visit with ease. At the end of each chapter an Additional Information section gives specific details such as addresses and opening times, making this guide a complete sightseeing companion. At the back of the guide the Fact File, arranged in alphabetical order, gives practical information and useful tips to help you plan your holiday — before you go and while you are there. The maps of each region show the main towns, villages, roads and places of interest, but are not designed as route maps and motorists should always use a good recommended road atlas.

INTRODUCTION

The Magic of Malta

With a climate warm and glowing for much of the year round, and enclosed by deep waters as clear and as blue as can possibly be imagined, Malta effortlessly enriches its visitors. Comprised of a cluster of small, rocky islands in the centre of the Mediterranean Sea, the sheer wealth of its attractions are truly overwhelming: sparkling swimming spots, riotously exuberant local festivals, historical sensations and so much more are all there to be enjoyed and experienced on an archipelago that on a map of the world, features as only the tiniest of dots.

Malta stands at the crossroads of the Mediterranean, looking north to Europe and south to Africa, and it is this geographical location, perfect for traders, that has endowed upon the island an historical significance that is far in excess of its diminutive size. Throughout every epoch of man's existence, there has been settlement on Malta. Prehistoric man was building both villages and immense temples on Malta over 1,000 years before the pyramids of Egypt were erected; St Paul was shipwrecked on the island only thirty years after the Crucifixion of Christ; in 1565 it was the base for staving off a tremendous assault by the Ottoman Empire which, had it succeeded, would have thrown open Southern Europe to the might of the Turkish Sultan's forces and, during World War II, its heroic resistance to one of the heaviest and most sustained bombing campaigns ever seen was to play a pivotal role in the final Allied victory. Phoenicians, Romans, Saracens, Normans, Spaniards, Frenchmen and Britons: all have left their mark on Malta and each one, in their own way, has added to the island's overall appeal. However, no occupier was to leave a greater stamp on Malta than the Knights of St John, an elite Christian Order composed of the noblest men in

Europe, men who were to fight ferociously and build prolifically.

Yet Malta has much more to offer than merely a heady and exciting history. Its fine climate and gorgeous waters have combined to turn the island into an ever increasingly popular hot-spot for tourists from across the globe. There are some lovely beaches here, some sandy, others rocky and the night life is varied enough to cater for all tastes, from quiet and traditional Maltese bars and restaurants to loud and modern clubs. Almost every type of water sport can be indulged and scuba divers in particular will find themselves in their element. Those who prefer a quieter holiday however, need not be put off the prospect of visiting Malta. The main bulk of the island's tourist industry — the hotels and apartment blocks, the souvenir shops and the more cosmopolitan restaurants — is centred on the northern coast, leaving much of the land blissfully quiet and un-spoiled: and for those who really want to enjoy a quiet and relaxing holiday, there is always either Gozo or Comino, satellite islands of Malta and each possessing their own, very special type of charm.

Being so small though, inevitably means that Malta does, in some ways, have its limitations and the visitor must be prepared for these. For example, there is no point in expecting an island filled with lavish forests and verdant fields — Malta is a hot and arid island with little in the way of flora and fauna: even trees are in extremely short supply. Do not anticipate beaches of the type that other Mediterra-nean countries possess, either. Although many of Malta's beaches are wonderful in their own right, they simply cannot compete with those found on nations such as Spain and Greece. Yet these are but trifling matters. Malta makes up for what it may lack, not least with the attitude of most of its people to their summer itinerants: for the Maltese are a kind and welcoming people who, by and large, treat holidaymakers courteously and with great friendliness. Besides, small is often beautiful for the visitor to Malta — nowhere is too far to travel to, and getting around the island is ridiculously easy.

Culturally, Malta is rich and vibrant. Throughout most of the year, fabulous *festas* are held in the villages, filling the night and the day with colour, music and dancing. Maltese food is in the process of a culinary comeback, and one could spend an entire holiday feasting on a different traditional dish each night. The medieval Manoel Theatre in the island's capital, Valletta, features an ongoing pro-gramme of music and drama that is varied and of the highest quality and a whole range of sporting activities are on offer, including those as diverse as clay pigeon shooting, archery and horse racing.

This guide contains all that one will need to enjoy a successful holiday on Malta. Each section of the island has been divided geographically, and detailed instructions take the reader-cum-visitor on each step of touring that section, be it a walking tour through the medieval streets of Valletta or Mdina, or a leisurely drive through the centre of the island, where the bulk of holidaymakers rarely venture. Local oddities are pointed out and discussed and where appropriate, each sight is set in its proper historical perspective. It also gives in abundance all sorts of indispensable advice, the sort of advice that makes the difference between a smooth and relaxed holiday and a fraught and frantic one: information such as from where to make an international telephone call, for example, or how to find a chemist that is open on a Sunday. In addition to this, this guide gives an account of the history of Malta, the reading of which will increase immeasurably one's understanding of the sights that are there to be marvelled at. Of course, one does not have to know who the Knights of St John actually were, or why the Turkish invasion of 1565 failed, or even what happened to St Paul during his unforeseen stay on the island, to enjoy a vacation here — but it certainly helps.

Geography and Geology

Malta is not one island but part of an archipelago of five, a cluster of tiny specks in the centre of the Mediterranean Sea that straddle the boundary between Europe and Africa. Largest and most populous of the group is Malta itself, followed by smaller Gozo to the west and the tiny Comino, in between the two. More miniscule still are Cominotto, off the coast of Comino, and Filfla, a guano-spattered rock south of the main island, both of which are uninhabited. The islands lie in a north-westerly, south-easterly direction 58 miles (93km) south of Sicily, 143 miles (230km) north of Libya and 181 miles (291km) east of Tunis.

Despite being queen of the group, Malta is a small island. Its dimensions, even at their widest points, measure only 17 miles (27km) by 9 miles (14km) and the length of its heavily serrated coastline is a mere 86 miles (138km). There are no mountains or rivers; rather, its landscape is characterised by low, green and brown hills, often terraced for agricultural purposes. There are several sandy beaches to the north-west.

Gozo is a greener, more fertile island, one that has been blessed with rugged good looks thanks to a rolling series of round, table-top hills. It is less than half the size of Malta — 9 miles (15km) long and 4 miles (7km) wide. Comino, where the longest distance in any direction is about a mile, has an arid, bumpy landscape. Despite its diminutive size, Comino is blessed with lots of enticing little coves and bays, and is very popular among water sports enthusiasts.

Contrary to popular belief, the Maltese islands are not volcanic. Geologically, they are mostly of limestone composition, the order of strata from the bottom up being: lower coralline limestone, globigerina limestone, blue clay, greensand and upper coralline limestone. It is the blue clay that gives the island's thin soil fertility.

History

MALTA THROUGH THE AGES

Malta has not always been an island. In the beginning, back in the days of the Ice Age, it was merely a mountain at the southern end of what is now Europe and was linked to that continent by a land bridge. This mountain was very different to the Malta of today. It was

A picturesque corner of Malta

larger, well-forested and lush; rivers gushed and wild animals roamed freely, unhindered by man who had not yet evolved. Then came the great thaw. The earth's climate warmed, the ice began its retreat to the poles and slowly the sea level rose. The mountain became an island, filled with those animals who had fled there from the ever encroaching waters, all fighting for what little food remained. This food could not last forever; the new, hot climate had parched the rivers and scorched the forests: the land was no longer lush and one by one, species by species, these animals were starved into extinction. It was the large creatures, those that needed the most food, who died first: the elephant, the hippopotami. They were followed by the smaller beasts; the deer, wolves and foxes: and in the end, it was only those that were either very small or very hardy — the reptiles, birds and small mammals — who survived.

MAN ON MALTA

Huge gaps exist in our knowledge of prehistoric man on Malta. All that is known is that which has been deduced by anthropologists and archaeologists from what these early communities have left behind. Much of what they did leave behind can still be seen today — huge megalithic temples, for example, and underground burial chambers

Malta is rich in prehistoric temples

— all of which point to one single, irrevocable, indisputable fact: that few other nations can boast a prehistory as ancient, as rich and as complex as the Maltese islands.

The first evidence of human habitation on Malta dates from around 5000BC. It is believed that man did not actually evolve here: rather, the early settlers came from elsewhere, presumably from Sicily, arriving on primitive boats and bringing with them all that they needed to build a new life here; livestock, for example, and seeds to grow crops. It was these people that laid the foundations of a prehistoric civilisation that was to last some 3,000 years. This civilisation passed through several stages in its development, stages that have been termed 'phases' in the language of archaeologists and, as remains of these first settlers have been found at Ghar Dalam, this earliest era has since become known as the Ghar Dalam Phase.

The Skorba Phase emerged around 4500BC. This takes its name from the settlement discovered at Skorba, near Mgarr, providing evidence of the houses that man then dwelled in: simple, round, stone-flagged huts. It was during this phase that the first temples began to be built.

The Ggantija Phase, dated to approximately 3800BC, represents a giant leap forward in man's development on Malta. Grand, huge temples were constructed, such as those unearthed at Hagar Qim and at Ggantija on Gozo. In themselves, these temples tell a tale of how advanced social organisation on the island had become. To build such temples must have required great planning — labourers, designers, stone-cutters, artists, site managers, and cooks, to name but a few — all would have been needed to mount such a vast operation, and in very large numbers. They also indicate the importance of religion on the island, a faith that was centred on the worship of fertility.

The next significant era was the Tarxien Phase of around 2900BC, named after the temples that have been discovered at Tarxien near Paola. Prehistoric man had developed further: the temples were smaller but more carefully planned, and bore a clearly superior standard of artwork and decoration. This too was the age of the hollowing out of the Hypogeum, a series of underground burial chambers near Tarxien that can still be visited today. Hints of the first arrival of the Bronze Age on Malta also date from this phase, in the finding of small, metal daggers presumably brought to the island from overseas.

Then, at some time between 2500BC and 1800BC, this entire civilisation simply vanished. Why it did is unknown and one of the great mysteries of Malta. It may have been plague or drought, or it may have been an invasion by a hostile force, although this latter explanation seems unlikely given the lack of any of the evidence that is normally found on battle sites. Either way the Maltese archipelago was deserted by man for some two centuries. In time, however, new settlers arrived, although little is known of them beyond that they had a small settlement near today's Borg-In-Nadur, and that they built a defensive wall there, and so presumably lived in fear of attack from some quarter.

Then, in around 1000BC, the Mediterranean began to blossom. New civilisations and cultures such as the Greeks and the Phoenicians emerged from the nations that flanked its shores. Trading boats began to criss-cross its waters and the strategic importance of Malta, the island that centred the sea, became recognised. In 800BC the greatest traders of them all, the Phoenicians, arrived from their colony of Carhage to colonise this island too.

PHOENICIAN RULE 800-218BC

The Phoenicians did build on Malta — a temple to their god on the Birgu promontory, for example — but for them the island was, as it was for the British some 3,000 years later, primarily a commercial centre, a safe harbour for their trading ships. The Greeks too used Malta for this purpose, although they presumably had to pay the Phoenicians for the privilege of doing so. Physically, almost nothing remains of the Phoenician's tenure on Malta although their prescence is evident in other ways — in the Maltese language, for example, which was originally based on the Phoenician tongue, and in the very name of the island itself, 'Malta' probably being a derivation of the Phoenician malat or 'harbour'. There are other theories: some say the name comes from the Greek *meli* which means 'honey', a produce for which Malta was then renowned. Gozo too, can claim Phoenician origins in its name: Gozo (spelt Ghawdex in Malti and pronounced 'Ow-desh') could be from the Greek *Gaudos* which could in turn be from the Phoenician *Gaulos,* which denoted a small type of Phoenican boat.

THE ROMANS ON MALTA 218BC-AD870

The Roman takeover of Malta seems to have been a peaceful one. Certainly there is no evidence that the islanders resisted this new power from the north; indeed, they may well have welcomed their new rulers. If this is the case, it could be the reason why Rome was not slow in granting *Melita*, as they called it, municipality status with the right to autonomy (under the eye of a Roman Governor, of course).

The early years of Roman rule were prosperous ones for Malta. Economically the island flourished as a harbour and as a producer of honey and evidence of such wealth can be seen in the remains of the Roman villa that was discovered in Rabat. Yet as the Roman Empire in the West faded, so too did Malta and the island entered into a long and bleak era in which it all but disappeared from history. Nominally ruled by the Eastern Roman Empire, it would have been in reality under the control of the Vandals who, as their name suggests, built and developed little. It was an age in which history stood still.

Nevertheless, it was during the Roman occupation that Malta became a Christian nation, and all because of a shipwreck off its northern coast in AD60. On board that ship was the evangelist Paul, on the way to his trial and subsequent execution in Rome. This unforeseen stop gave him the opportunity to evangelise some more, and to such good effect that he actually converted the island's Roman Governor, Publius, to the new faith and with him, most of the other islanders too. The apostle Luke, who was travelling with Paul, was impressed by the Maltese: 'After we had escaped (the shipwreck), we then learned that the island was called Malta. And the natives showed us unusual kindness....' (Acts 28:1-2)

ARAB RULE AD870-1090

By the mid-ninth century, all of North Africa was under the spell of the forces of Islam and it was inevitable that at some stage, demoralised and neglected Malta would also fall to this great new world power. In AD870, it did, and probably with the agreement of the islanders. Like the Romans before them, the Arabs felt no need to ravage the island and indeed proved to be tolerant rulers, particularly given the standards of the age. Sure, the Bishop of Malta was locked up and no new one appointed but the islanders still remained free to continue in their old, Christian faith. Many, however, decided to convert to Islam and it was not long before the island's Moslems outnumbered its Christians. Nevertheless, this era was not a happy time for Malta: the Arabs fortified Mdina in the form it retains today, but aside from that they built little and contributed less. Today, their most obvious legacy lies in the names of many Maltese towns and villages, many of which are of Arabic origin.

MEDIEVAL DAYS 1090–1530

Count Roger the Norman, the French ruler of Sicily, was a man keen to tighten his grip on that Italian island. This, however, he could not do as long as Arab forces existed in strength on Malta. It was because of this that he conquered the island in 1090 in a cunning pincer attack, half of his forces striking at St Paul's Bay, the other half at Dingli to the south. Tradition relates that upon victory Roger ripped off a piece of his red standard and gave it to the Maltese as a flag. The piece he gave them though, was too small and so the islanders increased its size by adding a white piece to it, thereby creating the red-and-white Maltese flag of today.

Norman rule brought changes to Malta. The Bishopric was reinstated, and a cathedral built in Mdina. Autonomy was granted to the islanders and a proper system of taxation and government installed. By the end of the twelfth century though, Malta was being passed around the various French, German and Spanish Counts and Royals who were jostling for control of Sicily. It was a time of flux for Malta, and a time in which an event occured that forever changed the character of the island: that was in 1250, when all of the island's Moslems were summarily expelled. Eventually, however, after a naval battle fought in Grand Harbour between the Spanish and the French, Malta came under the control of the Spanish Crown. The year was 1282.

Although the Spaniards appreciated Malta's usefulness as a trading post, they neglected the archipelago horribly. Little attempt was made to fortify the island and raids from corsairs (pirates) became a regular feature of life. The internal administration of the island fell to the Universita, a committee of Maltese noblemen based in Mdina. The only Spanish sovereign to visit the island during the entire 250 years of Spanish rule was Alphonso V and that was only to receive 30,000 florins from the Universita so that he could pay off a Spanish nobleman whom he had promised the island too. In return, Alphonso promised that Malta would forever remain the property of the Spanish Crown. One suspects that it was in spite of this, rather than because of it, that Alphonso gained his rather beatific epithet, 'the Magnanimous'.

THE KNIGHTS OF ST JOHN

Their origins were innocuous enough: a group of monks who called themselves the Hospitallers of St John of Jerusalem, and who had the sole purpose of caring for sick pilgrims who were visiting the Holy Land. Yet within 200 years these humble hospitallers had transformed themselves into the richest, noblest and most fearsome of all the religious Orders in Europe. How it happened is quite a story.

It all began when the monks widened their duties in the Holy Land to include escorting pilgrims on the final, most hazardous leg of their journey to Jerusalem. Their success in this earned them respect and prestige among holy men and soldiers alike and Knights from some of the noblest families in Europe applied to join them. This they were allowed to do providing they took the three vows of the Order — of poverty, chastity and obedience — and by 1113 these soldiers-cum-monks-cum-nurses had achieved full Order status, granted by the Pope.

The Knights flourished in the Holy Land until 1291 when they, along with the remainder of the Crusaders, were driven from the Holy Land by the Egyptian Mamluks. Casting around for a home, the Order briefly settled on Cyprus before being ousted from there also. It was only then, in 1310, that they set their sights on Rhodes and swiftly invaded and conquered this lovely Greek island, claiming it as their own. The Knights resided here for 212 years, an era in which they prospered immeasurably.

While maintaining their reputation as fine hospitallers and devout monks, it was on Rhodes that the Knights of St John also managed to amass tremendous wealth. It was not hard for them to do so. Such was its prestige that virtually every major and minor nobleman in Europe was eager to join them (no easy task: one had to prove seven successive generations of family nobility and also be prepared to take, and keep, the Order's vows), yet to do so one had to make an appropriate gift to the Order. Then, on the death of the Knight, all of his property (his estates in Europe, for example) would automatically revert to the Order, thus swelling the coffers further. Add to that the spoils gained from the regular raids that the Knights made on the Turkish coast and on Turkish shipping, and it is hardly surprising that the Order was said to have rivalled the Vatican in sheer wealth.

Socially, the Knights grouped themselves into *langues* 'languages', each *langue* representing a different nationality. There were eight such *langues*: of Provence, Auvergne, England, France, Germany, Leon and Portugal, Italy and Germany. Each *langue* would live communally, in an *auberge* or common house and each would have their own specific duties within the Order — the defence of a particular bastion, for example, or the responsibility for munition storage. The overall ruler was the Grandmaster, a man elected for life by all the Knights and who would rule as an absolute monarch.

Eventually the Turks tired of tolerating the infidel presence of the Knights on an island that was only two hours sailing from the Turkish coast. In 1522, under the direction of Sultan Suleiman the Magnificent, 200,000 Turkish troops set sail from Marmaris in over 400 ships to besiege the Knights, who were only 7,000 in number.

Nevertheless, the Knights held out for some six months before surrendering, and displayed such bravery that Suleiman granted them the right to leave unharmed, and to take with them their fleet and all their possessions. It was an act of a mercy the Sultan was later to regret.

The Baroque

The Knights of St John were great lovers of all that was flamboyant and exuberant, be that in architecture, art or music and so when the Baroque era swept the great cultures of Europe, they believed it to be a style tailor-made for themselves. Lasting from the early seventeenth to the early eighteenth centuries, the Baroque era was one in which simplicity and modesty were shamelessly banished, in favour of an art that was elaborate, decorative and assiduously detailed in all its forms. In music it involved composers such as Handel and Vivaldi and in art it encompassed such greats as Rubens and the volatile Caravaggio. Yet it is in architecture that the style persists most evidently in Europe today. World-famous structures such as the Palace of Versailles and London's St Paul's Cathedral are both fine examples of the Baroque at its best. Yet for sheer mile-for-mile density of examples of the style, few places are better than Malta.

Almost every building of any importance on Malta is built in Baroque. From the mid-seventeenth century onwards, the Knights not only built everything they could in this fashion, but also endeavoured to convert to it much of what had previously been built. Consequently, the Baroque can be seen everywhere, in churches adorned inside and out with intricate stonework and impossibly lavish furnishings and even in simple structures such as the façades of fountains, each with their stonework painstakingly carved in flowing twists and twirls. Ironically, given the loathing many of the Maltese had for the arrogant Knights, this is one area in which the Order's legacy still prevails on the archipelago: for the Maltese were infected with their enthusiasm for the Baroque and many of the buildings being erected today take a bow to this most extravagant of forms of design — as any visitor to the Church of St Joseph in Msida will see.

THE KNIGHTS OF ST JOHN ON MALTA 1530-1798

Finally, in 1529, the Spanish King Charles V hit upon a suitable use for Malta and offered it to the homeless Knights of St John, whom the Turks had expelled from Rhodes some seven years previously. The Knights sent out scouts to report on Malta who promptly brought back an account of an arid, poor island whose only attraction was a good harbour. Nevertheless, the Knights were not in a position to pick and choose and so they grudgingly accepted, much to the dismay of the Maltese nobility who foresaw, quite rightly as it turned out, their power on the island disappearing overnight. They too, however, had little choice in the matter and in 1530 the galleys of the Knights sailed in to Grand Harbour.

So as to be near their fleet (and away from the Maltese nobility) the Knights settled in Birgu, a promontory on the eastern side of Grand Harbour. Grand Master de l'Isle Adam installed himself in Fort St Angelo there, and immediately set about restoring the defences of this neglected city. He knew that the last thing that Sulieman, Sultan of Turkey, had wanted when he let the Knights leave Rhodes was that they would end up occupying the strategically most vital island in the Mediterranean, and thus stand between the Turks and their domination of the entire sea. This is what Charles V had planned.

The intricate beauty of the Baroque

Within fifteen years of the Knights arrival, sporadic raids on Malta by the Turks had begun, most of them led by Dragut, a grizzled old Turkish pirate from Bodrum who operated semi-independently of the Sultan. In 1546 Dragut all but destroyed Gozo, carrying most of its populace off into slavery and four years later, ravaged Malta leisurely while the Knights and the Maltese sheltered in furious impotence inside Birgu and Mdina. They knew that the big Turkish assault would not be long in coming. It was perhaps this that led the Knights to elect as Grandmaster in 1557 one of the Order's fiercest warriors, a man who had spent a year as a galley slave of the Turks and whom they knew would do all in his power to resist the Ottoman forces. His name was Jean de la Valette.

When the Turks eventually arrived, on 18 May 1565, it became clear that they were going to leave nothing to chance. To conquer this tiny island they brought a fleet of nearly 150 ships containing 40,000 men, many of them Janissaries, members of the Sultan's personal elite force. Their commander though, was to make an immediate critical error in judgement. Instead of launching a rapid attack on Birgu, which la Valette was still frantically fortifying, he decided to first take control of Grand Harbour and only then to attack Birgu. The advantage of this was that he could then attack the Knights in their capital by land and by sea; the disadvantage was that he first had to sieze Fort St Elmo, at the entrance to Grand Harbour. Dragut, who was to arrive nearly two weeks later with a force of 3,000 men and who was to take joint command of the assault, may well have questioned the wisdom of this approach. But Dragut was not yet there and by the time he was, the assault on St Elmo was well underway.

The battle for Fort St Elmo was hard, brutal and bitter. It took thirty-one critical days for the fort to fall, and although no defenders were to survive their deaths were ultimately the salvation of the Knights. Valette had sent emissaries to Sicily to plead for aid and although the Sicilians had agreed, they were still in the process of mustering a suitably strong force. Each day, therefore, was critical. For the Turks, however, St Elmo was a Pyrrhic victory. Not only did they lose 8,000 men in the assault but Dragut had been killed, slain by shrapnel.

Nevertheless, Grand Harbour was under their control and the battle for Birgu began in earnest. Volley after volley of Turkish cannonballs were hurled at the city and Knight and Turk locked in hand-to-hand combat. On one single day in July, the Turks lost over 2,500 men. Urged on by Valette, the Knights were resisting bravely but time was against them: their supplies of food and water were low and they were exhausted, sleep having become a luxury that none of them could afford. Yet the Turks were suffering too. Spanish galleys were sinking their supply ships that were leaving Tripoli, and their troops became weary and more demoralised by the day. The Turkish commander launched an assault on Mdina in the hope that this would re-vitalise his troops but this too, was repulsed.

Finally, on 7 September, a force of some 250 Sicilian Knights landed at Mellieha in relief of the Knights. This was a small force but to the Turks it spelt the end of their Malta adventure. Where some could come, they figured, more would surely follow. The following day the siege was lifted and from the ramparts of Birgu, the Knights watched in joy as the Turkish ships began their long voyage back to the Bosphorous to report their failure to the Sultan. They were never to return in force.

The Knights of St John however, did not know this. They immediately set about building a new capital, named Valletta after their heroic Grandmaster, on the promontory that split Marsamxett and Grand Harbours. Yet in addition, having fought for Malta, they took this island that they originally did not want, to their hearts. They fortified parts of the Maltese coastline, built sumptious churches across the island and traded heavily, exploiting the island's strategic position for trade to the full. Yet the islanders, who had fought equally bravely alongside the Knights during what became known as the Great Siege, found themselves increasingly alientated from the Order. The Knights were more concerned with ostentatious displays of wealth than they were for the welfare of the Maltese, whom they treated with little more than contempt. During the 268 years of the Knights rule on Malta, not a single Maltese was elected to the Order.

For an Order that had fought off the Turks with such vigour, it was ironic that the final death knell of the Knights was sounded far away from Malta, when in 1789 the Bastille in Paris was stormed and the French revolution began. The Order was at the time almost totally dominated by the French Knights, and financed by the vast estates of those Knights. With the arrival of a Republic in France however, all these estates were nationalised and the Order's funds evaporated. Eleven years later, when Napoleon's invasion fleet was sighted off the coast of Malta, Grandmaster Hompesch knew that his options had dwindled to nothing. In an ignominious end to a great Order, he surrendered Malta without a fight.

THE FRENCH OCCUPATION 1798-1801

With the possible exception of the British, the Maltese have never been well disposed to any of their occupiers. None were more hated, however, than the French. Their rule began well enough, the Maltese were glad to be rid of the overbearing and pompous Knights, but during the six days Napoleon spent on Malta, he wreaked more havoc on the island than the Knights had caused in 268 years. That French was decreed to be the official language was bad enough but worse was the shameless pillaging of the island. With the battle fleet of England's Horatio Nelson's bearing down on him, Napoleon needed funds fast and when he discovered that what he could take from the Maltese people's pockets was not enough, he robbed their treasures to make up the shortfall. The *Sacre Infirmia* of the Knights was looted mercilessly, all of its silver being stolen, as were the belongings of the Maltese nobility. Napoleon loaded the loot on board his flagship *Orient* and set sail to conquer Egypt, having first press-ganged hundreds of Maltese men into his army. Unfortunately for Napoleon, and ultimately for Malta too, he soon encountered Nelson's fleet at the mouth of the Nile delta and in the ensuing battle, a calamity for the French republic, the *Orient* went down with the treasures of Malta in it.

Consequently, Malta became an isolated French outpost. The French however, continued to plunder the island, a process that culminated in their attempt to auction off the treasures of the Carmelite Church of Our Lady in Mdina. For the devout Maltese, this was one act of sacrilege too many. The islanders rose in revolt, the French commander was hurled from a balcony in Mdina and the remainder of the French garrison barricaded themselves in Valletta. They stayed there for two years, while the Maltese fumed at the historical irony of it all, the only time that their impregnable capital had been besieged, and then by themselves! Nelson arrived to give advice and left a force under Captain Alexander Ball to blockade Malta but eventually, no attack was needed. Starvation was what drove the French troops out.

In the two years Ball had blockaded Valletta, he had forged good links with the Maltese and, after the last French soldier had left, the Maltese agreed to accept Ball as their temporary Governor. It was a measured move. Britain and France were still at war and one of the greatest prizes that victory could offer either of them was control of Malta. Having accepted that they would not be masters of their own destiny, the Maltese realised that they must side with a power that would best suit their interests; and having tasted French rule once, they had no desire to repeat the experience. In the event, they had no need too: the French were finally defeated at Waterloo in 1815 and that same year, the Congress of Vienna confirmed Malta as a British colony.

MALTA AS A BRITISH COLONY

There can be little doubt that Britain brought a new prosperity to Malta: trade flourished, the shipyards and harbours were used to full effect, even a railway line was built. There again, it was not for love of the Maltese that the British did this. For this great sea power, Malta was quite simply the most important outpost in the Mediterranean and consequently, it had to be nurtured. The islanders did receive some measure of autonomy following World War I although internal clashes between the British authorities and the Catholic Church led this to be suspended in 1936. Besides, at this time both the British and the Maltese had a far greater concern to occupy themselves with — the rise of fascist Germany and, only a few hours sailing from the Maltese shores, Italy.

THE SECOND SIEGE OF MALTA 1940-43

Despite the strategic importance of Malta, Britain left the island all but undefended for the first year of the war. This was a testing time for the UK. France had been lost and London and other major cities were being pounded nightly by the *Luftwaffe*. Scenting a quick German victory, Mussolini decided to get on the Nazi's bandwagon. On 10 June 1940 he declared Italy to be at war with the Allied powers. The following day Italian aircraft attacked Malta. It was an attack that marked the beginning of the second Great Siege of Malta, a siege as courageous, and as ultimately victorious, as the one fought against the Turks some 365 years before.

The siege lasted from that day to the end of September 1943, the Axis powers determined to sieze the island, the Allied powers equally determined to hold it. For either, the rewards for victory were immense; at the very least, the victor could enjoy unhindered control of the entire Mediterranean arena and by extension, of North Africa and the route to India. Thus it was that Malta, to many commentators the 'Mediterranean's unsinkable aircraft carrier', became the stage for a battle that neither side could afford to lose. Nevertheless, there was no physical invasion of the island. Rather this was a battle fought in the air and on the sea, between the Hurricanes of the RAF and the *Stukas* of the *Luftwaffe*, and between the German U-boats and the British merchant vessels. For the German strategy was to simply pound and starve the Maltese people into submission.

In order to achieve this the Axis powers launched the most ferocious, the most sustained bombing campaign of World War II, and coupled it with a complete naval blockade of the island. The statistics attached to this are astonishing. During three years, from June 1940 to September 1943, the Axis powers launched no less than 3,332 raids on Malta, most of them directed at Grand Harbour and the docklands, dropping a total of over 16,000 tons of bombs. In April 1942, when the battle for Malta was at its height and the islanders morale at its lowest, nearly 7,000 bombs were dropped at an average of 230 a day by aircraft attacking in numbers of 200 or more. Great chunks of Valletta and the 'three cities' of Senglea, Vittoriosa and Cospicua were pulverised. Yet that was not all. The Axis's naval blockade of the island proved equally telling. Ships steaming in convoys to re-supply Malta with food, oil and munitions were frequently sunk within hours of leaving port and many of those that made it to Grand Harbour were sunk by dive-bombers even as they were being unloaded. Strict rationing was introduced and yet still the Maltese staggered defiantly on, hungry and exhausted, as their

Malta's citation for the George Cross, the Grand Masters' Palace, Valletta

island was systematically destroyed about them. These were terrible years for Malta yet in retrospect they were proud years too, and ones epitomised by the citation that accompanied the George Cross awarded to Malta by King George VI in April 1942: 'To honour her brave people I award the George Cross to the island fortress of Malta to bear witness to a heroism and devotion that will long be famous in history'. The George Cross is Britain's highest award for civilian gallantry. Neither before or since has it been awarded to the people of an entire nation.

Malta was never to fall to the Nazi's and its resistance was undoubtedly a major factor in turning the tide of war against the Axis powers and in favour of the Allies. Montgomery's 8th Army overwhelmed Rommel's *Afrika Korps* at El Alamein and a successful invasion of Sicily was launched from Malta. Eventually on 8 September 1943 Admiral Cunningham, Commander-in-Chief Mediterranean fleet cabled the following message to London: 'Be pleased to inform their lordships that the Italian battle fleet now lies at anchor under the guns of the fortress of Malta'.

THE POST-WAR YEARS AND THE ROAD TO INDEPENDENCE

In the years following World War II, Great Britain offloaded its colonies but showed a marked disinclination to dispense with Malta. The Maltese people had no objection to this and indeed, by 1956 ties with Britain were so strong that a referendum was held on the subject of whether the island should fully unite with the mother country, and send three Maltese members to the House of Commons. Prime Minister Dom Mintoff of the Malta Labour Party was enthusiastic about the plan but Malta's Roman Catholic Church was not. Amidst political turmoil, they called for a boycott of the referendum and nearly 50 per cent of the electorate followed this lead. The plan for union died and the long running strife between Malta's Labour Party and the Church was born.

In 1964 the Nationalist Prime Minister Dr Borg Olivier, with Labour Party backing, declared Malta to be an independent member of the British Commonwealth. This, however, was not enough for the people of an island that had been dominated by foreign powers ever since the boats of the Phoenicians first landed on its shores some 3,000 years before. Ten years later Malta declared itself a neutral Republic, with a Maltese President replacing the British Crown as the Head of State. Five years after that, the last British warship left Grand Harbour. Malta had finally cut its links with a past which had seen it entirely subjugated to the rule of others. At long last, it was free to make its own way in the world.

Food and Drink

Unlike many of the other nations of the Mediterranean, Malta does not enjoy a reputation as a purveyor of fine cuisine. Neither, however, is it as bad as some have suggested and stories of Maltese food being little more than an unholy combination of British and Italian cooking at their very worst are today, thankfully, false. Nevertheless, to enjoy a good meal one has to pick a restaurant carefully; all too many still seem to be under the misapprehension that the island is still full of British sailors and specialise only in a sorry and soggy menu of burgers, eggs, and chips which, if you are not here to sample local culinary delights, is fine. Other restaurants however, are more enterprising and have returned to serving their customers what the average citizen of Malta has been enjoying for years: traditional Maltese food, much of which is superb. Many of these restaurants are mentioned within this guide, others are easy enough to find as they tend to advertise themselves well, having placards outside with legends such as 'Maltese Home Cooking' emblazoned upon them.

Maltese food, like the Maltese language, is a mish-mash of the various races and cultures that have imposed themselves on the island over the centuries. The most obvious sources for many of the meals are the Knights of St John. Each *auberge* would have had its own chef, most probably from that *langues* country of origin, who would have cooked their favourite dishes from home. These chefs would have had Maltese helpers, recipes would have been swapped, experiments made and a whole new cuisine emerged, distinctly local but with its roots in Northern Europe. Consequently, several Maltese dishes are simply variations on an established theme. *Toqlija*, for example, is ratatouille under another name. Likewise *Torta tal-Haxu*, which would be called Quiche Lorraine anywhere else on the continent. With Sicily being little more than a few hours sailing away though, it is the Italian influence that is the strongest, *Ravjul* (ravioli) being a popular item on many a menu. For other, more traditionally Maltese meals, one could sample any one of the following:

Stuffat tel-Fenek: if there is such thing as a Maltese national dish then this is it. Rabbit fried in a wine and tomato sauce and served with spaghetti or pasta; *Hut Biz-Zalza:* usually delicious. This is fish (often lampuki) served in a sauce of tomatoes and what is a common ingredient in Maltese cooking, capers; *Minestra:* minestrone soup, but always including pumpkin and pasta; *Timpana:* a baked macaroni pie, with meat and eggs; *Bragioli:* eggs, bacon, mincemeat, olives and breadcrumbs, encased in rolls of thin steak; *Brungiel:* aubergines, stuffed with whatever is nearest to hand — mincemeat, tomatoes, etc; *Ross il-Forn:* baked rice, cooked with mincemeat, eggs and cheese.

Malta is a good place for snacks. Burgers and chips can be bought anywhere but for something more authentic, opt for *pastizzi*, small pasties filled with either cheese or peas. They are very tasty and very cheap and for the traveller on a limited budget, two or three make for a perfectly adequate meal. Picnickers will enjoy the crusty Maltese bread and possibly the local cheeses too, which are made from sheeps milk. The most common type of cheese is *Gbejna* and devotees of cottage cheese will probably want to try *rikotta*, too. A dessert in Malta is likely to be either ice-cream or fresh fruit. Those who like the idea of a sweet of frittered dates however, may want to ask for *mqaret*, although it is not always that easy to find.

Breakfast, alas, is not considered to be a particularly important meal by the Maltese and in most hotels, guests will in the morning be confronted with only a cup of tea or coffee, and a roll with jam or marmalade.

Before the British arrived and introduced beer to Malta the traditional tipple of the islanders was wine. The colonisers, however, could not quite eradicate the fondness of the Maltese for the grape and today, wine-making still flourishes on Malta. Prices are cheap and the quality, as a rule, is very good, especially the reds which seem

Market traders waiting for customers

to have a particularly silky texture. Maltese grapes grow close to the ground, thus producing a smaller and sweeter fruit that when fermented, can result in an extremely potent concoction. Gozitan wine has a flavour that is best described as unique — try it and you will see why.

Beer drinkers can choose from a range of imported beers, but why bother when the local brew is cheaper and equally good? Farsons, the island's brewery, has been in the business of beer production for generations, using hops imported from Kent and Worcestershire, and its two big sellers, Hop leaf and Blue Label, offer as good a pint as can be found anywhere. The company was hit hard by the departure of the Royal Navy from the island: in 1974, a full 20 per cent of Farson's annual production was sold to Naafi for consumption by the British servicemen.

Hopleaf Pale Ale, a popular thirst-quencher for locals and visitors alike

Aside from the usual soft drinks there is also Kinnie which is fizzy, locally made and flavoured with oranges and aromatic herbs. As a thirst-quencher, Kinnie is hard to beat but if it does not come ice cold and served with a slice of lemon, then send it back (the Maltese do). It tastes pretty good as a mixer for spirits, too.

Plants and Wildlife

Both flora and fauna find it hard to flourish on the Maltese archipelago. The limestone base of the islands makes it hard for plants to take root, an effect worsened by the punishing north-westerly wind that blows what topsoil there is away. Nowhere on the islands is more than 4 miles (6km) from the sea so anything that does grow has to be salt-water resistant. Add all of this to the fact that most available space on the islands is taken up by the needs of man, in the form of either building or farming, and one can see that Malta is not a nation likely to delight the amateur naturalist.

Back in the midsts of prehistoric Malta, the land was rich in both plants and animals. The weather was much wetter and cooler then, and even beasts as large as the elephant and the hippopotamus found enough vegetation to thrive for millennia. Even up to the eighteenth century there were certain animals indigenous to the island such as wild boar and rabbit but these too have now disappeared, thanks mainly to the various Grandmasters love of hunting and the Maltese's love of fried rabbit. Consequently, only the smallest and hardiest of creatures — lizards, for example — survive today. One would expect a good deal of migratory bird life on the archipelago, given the fact that Malta is a bridging point between cold Europe and warm Africa, but sadly this is not the case. Besides, any migrant birds that linger too long on the island tend to be trapped by the locals.

Gozo, however, does have a domestic animal that it can call its very own. This is the *kelb tal fenek*, the 'rabbit hound', said by many to be directly related to the hounds of the Egyptian Pharoahs, and first brought to the island by the Phoenicians.

Outside official gardens such as those at the San Anton Palace and the Argotti in Floriana, trees are in short supply, particularly along the wind-buffeted northern coast. Carob trees, however, with their great spreading branches swooping darkly down to the ground (traditionally, a good hiding spot for young lovers) can be seen in the south, and fruit trees too, although these have been imported so as to take good advantage of Malta's Mediterranean climate. Indeed, much of what would have been fertile ground for indigenous plants and trees has been given over to those that will serve the interests of farming, and one will see fields of grapes, and potatoes, among other crops. One can find a few European oaks too, amidst the pines at the Buskett Gardens south of Mdina. A few olive trees still persist, although what commercial value they possessed has long since passed.

Some plants are quite common, most notably the hardy tamarisk, which has deep roots and grows close to the ground, and which favours a shoreside location. Also common are capers, which grow among the ruins of old fortifications and buildings and which the Maltese turn into a delicious sauce. Orchids can be plentiful during the spring months of February to April but one has to look hard to find them: try hunting around rocky plateaux, or on the slopes of valleys.

Population, Politics and the Economy

When the galleys of the Knights of St John first sailed into Grand Harbour in 1530, Malta's populace numbered only a paltry 15,000. Since then, however, the Maltese have proved themselves to be masters of procreation: over 360,000 people live in the archipelago today thus making it, in proportion to its size, one of the most densely populated countries in the world. Of these, roughly 10,000 live in Valletta (there would undoubtedly be more if available space in the city was not so limited) and approximately 190,000 in the inner and outer suburbs of the capital, in towns such as Hamrun and Sliema. Gozo's population is comparatively small at approximately 26,000, but even this is 25,997 more than those that live on Comino.

Part of the pleasure of visiting Malta is meeting the Maltese. Generally speaking, they are a quiet, devout and welcoming race with a decidedly conservative outlook on life that some would praise as worthy and others deride as old-fashioned. It is certainly true that various conventions that are acceptable in 'the west' are firmly frowned upon here: gambling, for example, and topless sunbathing. The nations crime rate is low and social problems such as drug abuse are rare. The Roman Catholic Church, to which the vast majority of the islanders adhere, still exerts a powerful influence. Visitors would do well to respect this and to dress and act appropriately while in a church, ie to behave in a quiet, decorous fashion and to dress modestly, with legs and arms fully covered. The Maltese are a tolerant race but draw the line at their hospitality being abused in this way.

Yet first and foremost the Maltese are a proud people. The island-ers speak of their courageous past with self-satisfied relish, although such pride can often be mingled with disgruntlement at having been ruled for so long by foreign powers. It is perhaps because of this that they can be rather sensitive to criticism, particularly if that criticism comes from a quarter that they would traditionally expect support from.

Politics is a subject very dear to the Maltese heart. Having been denied self-governance for so long, the islanders now take a positive delight in hurling themselves whole-heartedly into the democratic process, and the rights and wrongs of various policies and politicians provide a never-ending source of debate in the nations restaurants and bars. Support for the two major political groupings, the left-wing Labour Party and the right-wing Nationalist Party, is divided roughly equally among the populace although it is the Nationalists who are currently in the ascendancy. They have been so since the May 1987 elections when they won a victory that ended sixteen years

The focal point of the festa, *carrying the saint's statue out of the church*

of continuous Labour Party rule.

Since opting for independence in 1974, the British Monarch has been supplanted by the Maltese President as the island's Head of State. Like a monarch however, the President's duties are largely ceremonial, and include tasks such as greeting esteemed visitors, and appearing on bank notes looking suitably statesmanlike. National elections are held every five years to elect members of Malta's unicameral Parliament, the House of Representatives, and it is these Representatives who in turn elect a Cabinet, which is where real political power resides. It is an experience to be in Malta during the run-up to a general election, when feelings and emotions run dizzily high and when a noisy rally seems to be held on every other street corner. Given this, it is hardly surprising that the island has one of the world's highest turn-out rates for elections — a remarkable 97 per cent of the electorate vote, as compared to roughly 75 per cent in the UK and little more than 50 per cent in the USA.

The British dockyards that the Maltese nationalised in 1973 still provide the mainstay of the island's economy, working in ship repair and ship building. With seven drydocks and over 1 mile (nearly 2km) of available berthage, the docks service an average of some 250 vessels a year, and appear to have managed to retain their fair share of what is an increasingly competitive market in Europe. Smaller boats are serviced in the Manoel Island Yacht Yard. Light industry has been successful in establishing itself on the island and food exports, most notably potatoes to the Netherlands, have begun. Although like much of Europe, Malta has been hurt economically by the recession of the early 1990s, it still can boast a high degree of economic competence: indeed, between 1963 and 1983 the nation enjoyed the highest recorded growth rate in terms of real Gross National Product per head of population than any other country in the world.

Malta's biggest trading partners today are two of its closest neighbours, Italy and Libya. It is the latter who, grateful for a friend in the west, provides the island's oil. Closer links have recently been forged with the EEC and so in the future, the markets open to Malta will widen. It is, however, tourism that is the biggest earner of much-coveted foreign currency. Approximately 870,000 visitors entered Malta in 1990: nearly two-and-a-half times more than there are Maltese.

1

VALLETTA

A relative newcomer to the capitals of Europe, Valletta was born out of the Knight's victory in the Great Siege of 1565. Prior to that it was just Mount Sciberras, a barren, rocky tongue of land protruding between Marsamxett Harbour and Grand Harbour. This promontory, undefended except for Fort St Elmo at its tip, had been seized by the Turks during the siege so that the Ottoman fleet could gain access to the sheltered waters of Marsamxett Harbour. The Turks though, soon discovered that control of Sciberras held additional advantages. The promontory was situated higher than the Knights capital city of Birgu, which stood across the waters of Grand Harbour, and its peak made the ideal gun emplacement from which to rain cannon fire down upon the entrapped defenders. By the time the siege was lifted in September 1565, Grandmaster Jean de La Valette had vowed that never again would a hostile force be allowed to take control of Sciberras. He gave orders that Birgu be replaced as the island's capital by a new, heavily fortified city that was to be built atop the mount and although La Valette was to die before this city could be completed, it seemed only right that it should be named for him.

Few cities are visually more striking. Indeed, visitors travelling to Malta by air would be well advised to sit on the left side of the aeroplane when arriving, and on the right side when departing, so as to best appreciate the spectacular collection of promontories, harbours and creeks that comprise Valletta and its surrounds. On the ground too, it is hard not to be immediately impressed, particularly by ones first view of the walls. Immense in height and breadth, and bolstered by huge demi-bastions and protruding ravelins, they were completed within five years, breakneck speed by the standards of the day, on the orders of Knights fearful that the Turks would soon return to seek vengeance. Only when the walls were completed could work begin on the city's interior, designed by the Pope's personal architect, Laparelli, and modelled on the then newly-built city of Lisbon. As with the Portuguese capital, Laparelli laid out Valletta's streets in todays grid-plan fashion, building in what were then new and revolutionary sewerage and drainage systems that were to make the city the most technically advanced of its day.

When Laparelli returned to Rome, his work was continued by the Maltese architect Gerolamo Cassar, the man who was to be responsible for many of the most elegant edifices of Valletta. Money was no object for Cassar: the crowned heads of Europe, grateful to the Knights for saving Southern Europe from the spectre of Ottoman domination, were prepared to donate as much as was needed. Over the years, Cassar's work was enlarged and adorned on the orders of Grandmasters attracted by the Baroque anelaborate, highly decorative architectural style that was so popular in Europe in the late seventeenth century. Now, almost every street in the city carries examples of the Baroque that can be seen in the grandiose adornments, carved cornices and exquisitely designed portals of its most significant structures. It became a city rich in many ways, one that the British Prime Minister Disraeli claimed was '...a city built by gentlemen, for gentlemen.'

During World War II the bombs of the *Luftwaffe*, while managing to destroy great chunks of the city, could not quite do their worse. Much of old Valletta remained intact and today, this makes the city a magnet for sight-seers. Shoppers too, will enjoy Valletta. All of the

MAP KEY

TOUR 1•REPUBLIC STREET

1   Church of St Francis of Assissi
2   Church of St Barbara
3   Sapienzas
4   Auberge of the Knights of Provence/National Museum of Archaeology
5   Bank of Valletta
6   St John's Co-Cathedral/Museum
7   Law Courts
8   National Library of Malta
9   Grand Masters' Palace/Armoury Museum
10 Wartime Experience
11 Casa Rocca Piccola
12 Church of Our Lady of Damascus

TOUR 2•THE CITY WALLS

13 Church of Our Lady of the Victory
14 Church of St Catherine
15 Palazzo Parisio
16 Castellania
17 Church of St Paul's Shipwreck
18 Malta Siege Memorial
19 Hospital of the Knights of St John
20 National War Museum
21 Church of Our Lady of Mount Carmel
22 Manoel Theatre
23 St Andrew's Scottish Church
24 National Museum of Fine Arts

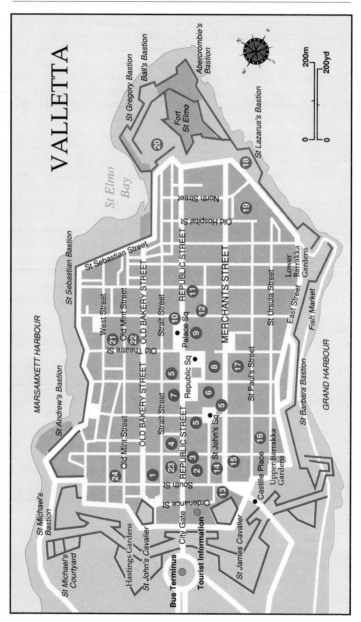

Valletta's skyline

*Parking can be a
problem in Valletta*

traditional Maltese souvenirs can be purchased here — the glass-ware, the lace, the knitted sweaters, and so on — either in the shops or in the street market (mornings only) held from Monday to Friday on Merchants Street. On Sunday mornings, outside the city walls near the bus terminus, another street market is held, one primarily aimed at tourists and specialising, in the main, in pirated video and cassette tapes. Valletta has plenty of snack bars and pubs and a fair number of quality restaurants too, several of which are named in this chapter. Places to stay, however, can be rather thin on the ground. There are a handful of guest houses, and several accredited hotels, but little at the top end of the range; a full list of accommodation available in the city can be obtained from the tourist office. Swim-mers should note that although Valletta has no beach, it is still possible to take a dip in Grand Harbour, off the white rocks below the Mediterranean Conference Centre near St Lazarus's Bastion.

The city is best explored on foot rather than by private car. Firstly, because some of the most interesting streets are accessible only on foot and secondly, because, finding parking space can be a fearful problem (and Valletta's traffic wardens are particularly zeal-ous). Finding ones way around should rarely be a problem thanks to the modern, Euro-American grid plan lay-out and the fact that all streets are clearly marked. Anyone who does get lost should merely cut inland, wherever they happen to be; by doing this they will eventually arrive at Republic Street, the main thoroughfare that cuts through the centre of the city, and from there be able to re-orientate themselves. The thought of seeing an entire capital city on foot need not be unnecessarily daunting: Valletta, although very hilly, is small, its walls having prevented any outward expansion. Besides, the exhausted can always make use of the city's most conspicuous transport system, that age old horse and carriage, the *karrozzin*.

Note that although Valletta is lively in the mornings and around lunchtime, it quietens down considerably after approximately 1.30pm when most of the shops and many of the museums close for a lengthy afternoon *siesta*. The majority of the restaurants do open again for the evening trade but there is little entertainment beyond these. If it is nightlife you are after, go to Sliema or St Paul's.

Outlined below are two walking tours of Valletta. One follows Republic Street, taking in the better known of the edifices and sights. The other is a little more off-beat, following the city walls around the edges of Grand and Marsamxett Harbours to discover some of the less well-known, but equally intriguing, attractions of the city. Taking it slowly, beginning early and finishing at around lunchtime, allocate one day for each walk although those in a hurry may be able to complete both in a day. Both walks begin at Valletta's bus terminus, located just outside the city gate, from where there are regular connections to and from all points on Malta.

Tour One • Republic Street

Valletta's main gate is a poor introduction to a city that is otherwise so architecturally impressive. This gate, the fourth that Valletta has seen on this site, was built in the 1960s to a plain, cumbersome and overbearing design and scarcely merits even a photograph. What can be enjoyed, however, is the approach to the gate, across a concrete walkway that bridges the immense dry ditch of Valletta. Looking over the walls of the walkway, which is flanked by two gigantic demi-bastions, it is easy to appreciate the superb defences of the city. The ditch, not a moat as it was never filled with water, is 18m (60ft) deep and 9m (30ft) wide and, stretching as it does from Marsamxett Harbour to Grand Harbour, completely seals the city off from the rest of Malta, thus making Valletta an island in itself.

Through the city gate is Freedom Square. Immediately to the right is the city's tourist office. Across the square is the site of what was once the Royal Opera House, said by many to have been Valletta's most beautiful building until German bombs pulverized it one day in April 1942. Now only the site and a few crumbling arches remain, while a debate still rages in Malta as to what to do with such prime real estate. On the right hand side of the square, a series of shops marks the one-time site of Valletta railway station, closed in 1932, while straight ahead directly opposite city gate, Republic Street begins.

Arrow-straight, supremely elegant and almost one mile (1 ½ km) in length, Republic Street splits the city in two, running across the old peak of Mount Sciberras before eventually descending to Fort St Elmo at the tip of the promontory. Despite its status as the main thoroughfare of a capital city, Republic Street is remarkably quiet: except for two hours in the afternoon, much of its length is closed to traffic daily, and then is open for delivery trucks only.

One of the foremost features of Republic Street are its balconies and indeed, it is these that are the first to catch the eye upon entering the street. Overhanging and carefully decorated, these balconies of wood and stone can be seen all over the island but here they seem particularly impressive, resembling a collection of elaborate, green-painted window boxes. Note that many of their windows are louvred — that is, that the windows are comprised of wooden panels with slits cut horizontally across them, a style developed by the Arabs which allowed their women to look out onto the street, but which prevented passers-by in the street looking in at their women.

A few steps down the street, two 'minor sights' immediately present themselves, the **Church of St Barbara** and the **Church of St Francis of Assissi**. Mass is said in English every Sunday and on public holidays at the eighteenth-century Church of St Barbara, which is the plainer of the two and was once the property of the Knights of Provence. The Church of St Francis bears more than a few traces of the Baroque, with its wide altar dominated by seven huge candlesticks and a ceiling decoratively gilt-edged. Indeed its most impressive feature, is on the ceiling; an immense, yet very gentle, painting of Christ in heaven. Further on from this church is Sapienzas, an excellent book shop with a wide selection of English-language books on Maltese history and culture.

The *auberge* of the Knights of Provence, one of the first buildings designed by Cassar for Valletta, is a short walk down from Sapienzas. This is now the home of the **National Museum of Archaeology**, with several rooms devoted solely to artefacts unearthed from the prehistoric sites of Malta. Taking pride of place are the finds from Tarxien, relics from an era that represented the height of the Copper Age civilisation, and including the legs and balloon-shaped torso that once formed part of a statue of a fertility goddess that would have stood over 2m (7ft) high. There are blocks and stones

The remarkable wooden balconies of Valletta

engraved with the decorative horned spirals that were so typical of the age and, in the corner of the room, a sacrificial altar. The statue, the stones and the altar are all original, having been removed from the site (and subsequently replaced with replicas) to protect them from further weather erosion. From Hagar Qim there is a large limestone altar, beautifully adorned with a tree in relief. Other rooms contain shards of pottery, small tools, figurines, skulls, bowls and other remnants of an era about which precious little is known. The displays are effectively laid out and well labelled but if possible, try to see some of the prehistoric sites themselves before seeing the museum; what is on show will then have a good deal more meaning.

Leaving the Archaeology Museum and continuing down Republic Street, one passes the Bank of Valletta and then the King's Own Restaurant, an eatery a good deal better than its rather sorry appearance would suggest. It is a friendly place, lively in the evenings and reasonably priced. Just after the restaurant, leave Republic Street to turn right into St John's Street and enter St John's Square. This is the place to find one of the archaeological wonders of Valletta, indeed of Malta as a whole: **St John's Co-Cathedral**.

First appearances, however, would suggest that this is not much of a wonder. It was built by Cassar in plain, Mannerist style back in the days when the church was the last refuge of a city's defenders and accordingly, was constructed with defence in mind as much as religious worship. There are very few windows at its lower levels and what there are are tiny and barred and impossible to even squeeze through. It does have a carved stone balcony above the main entrance, from which the election of a new Grandmaster was announced, and a clock tower which bears not one clock but three: one for the time, one for the date and the other for the day. Either side of the entrance are two huge bronze cannons, which date back to the days of the Knights. Yet it is the interior that makes the Co-Cathedral the marvel that it is; for this is a church that has been constructed in one style yet stunningly re-designed into another; the Baroque.

The re-design was the work of the seventeenth-century Italian artist Mattia Preti and upon entering the church, the sheer splendour of his creation leaves one baffled as to what to look at first. Above there is the barrel-vaulted ceiling, into which Preti has cut circular windows so as to best illuminate the light, colourful paintings that cover every spare inch of it; the paintings depict the life of John the Baptist and all come from the brush of Preti himself. Below, one walks on tombstones, each one displaying in bright mosaic the coat of arms of the Knight or Bishop that lies below. Over 400 Knights are buried here. The walls are carved in high relief, with swirling and graceful designs. It is an awesome church, one that unapologetically revels in its magnificence.

Despite its finery though, St John's is not the cathedral of Malta. That honour belongs to St Paul's Cathedral in Mdina which has holy connotations in that it was built on the alleged site of the house of Publius, the Roman Governor whom Paul converted to Christianity and who was subsequently martyred. Malta is a small diocese and as such, is only allowed one cathedral. In deference to the importance of St John's though, it was granted Co-Cathedral status, making it almost a cathedral but not quite.

St John's is built to a simple rectangular design, with side aisles either side containing a series of chapels. Each *langue* claimed a chapel as its own, and each one has its own curiosities. It is by visiting these chapels in turn that one can best view the Co-Cathedral.

Before seeing the chapels though, take a look at the tomb of the Italian Grandmaster Zondadari, constructed in heavy Baroque and positioned to the left of the main entrance. Some Grandmasters preferred to be buried simply but Zondadari was not one of them. His huge and elaborate statue, positioned atop the tomb, features crucifixes to indicate that he was a pious man, weapons to show that he had won many battles and an anchor, in order to mark his rank as Admiral of the Knights Galleys. Throughout the era of the Knights, the Italian *langue* maintained control of the Order's fleet.

The first of the chapels is small and contains little of interest save for the tombstone of Preti (although it is hard to spot which one is his) and a statue of Christ, flanked by the Virgin and the Magdalene. Better is the adjacent chapel of Germany, dedicated to the Magi and floored with the tombstones of German knights. The chapel was originally alloted to the English *langue*: the Knights were for years hopeful that England would re-convert to Catholicism and that the English *langue*, dissolved by Henry VIII, would return to the Order. By the end of the seventeenth century though, it had become clear that this was merely a pipe dream and the chapel was claimed by the German *langue*. The crest above the chapel's altar is of red and white, the old colours of Germany and ones that are today used by Austria.

Grandmaster Nicolas Cotoner was the financier of the next chapel and like a latter-day graffiti artist, his initials are carved in relief all over the walls together with his symbol, the cotton plant. This was perhaps in imitation of his elder brother and predecessor as Grandmaster, Rafael, whose own 'RC' initials plaster the walls of the adjacent chapel, that which belonged to the *langue* of Italy. There is a fine altar in this chapel, one designed by Preti and called *The Mystic Marriage of St Catherine*, as well as a masterly bust of Grandmaster

Carafa but the chief prize here is a painting of St Jerome by the great Italian artist, Caravaggio. Caravaggio's relationship with the Knights of St John was brief and, like the man himself, tempestuous and is worth relating here.

He first came to Malta in 1607 after the Knights had decided to commission an artist to paint a depiction of the beheading of John the Baptist. Unfortunately, no artist suitably illustrious was available at the time but an Italian Knight, who had heard of Caravaggio's skills, sang his praises and was duly despatched to Rome to find him. Caravaggio though, was not there; he had fled the city as he was wanted there for murder. Not to be deterred, the Knight eventually tracked him down to Naples where he conveyed to the fugitive the Grandmaster's offer: if Caravaggio would come to Malta to undertake the painting, he would be made a Knight of St John. This was an offer impossible to refuse, even for a character as difficult as Caravaggio. To be a Knight, one normally had to prove a nobility that spanned back seven generations. This was an easy way in to the most esteemed Order in Europe. It also offered the artist something in which he was sorely lacking, namely respectability.

So Caravaggio came to Malta, was made a Knight and duly completed four paintings, of which St Jerome was one and the Beheading of John the Baptist the other. He also managed to pick a quarrel with a Knight which eventually resulted in him beating the unfortunate fellow half to death. The artist was thrown into jail but with outside help, managed to escape and flee the island whereupon the Knights, glad to be rid of such a troublesome individual, wasted no time in expelling him from their Order and declaring him *persona non grata* on Malta. Besides, they had their painting.

Four Grandmasters are buried in the Chapel of France, which is next to that of Italy, but otherwise this chapel holds little of interest. The following chapel however, once the preserve of the Knights of Provence, has a marvellous titular painting of St Michael above the altar and monuments dedicated to the memories of Grandmasters de Paule and Castellar. Adjoining Provence is a small chapel, that of the Holy Relics, allocated to the Bavarians who, together with a handful of English Catholics, were given their own *langue* in the late eighteenth century. The wooden statue of St John that is displayed here is said to be carved from wood from the ship that carried Grandmaster de L'Isle Adam from Rhodes.

From the chapel of Provence, a short flight of steps leads down to the crypt, sealed off by an iron grille that is opened only on All Souls Day on the 2 November. Several Grandmasters are buried here but peering through the grille, only the tombs of two can be clearly discerned. The sarcophagus directly ahead belongs to de L'Isle Adam, the last Grandmaster of Rhodes and the first of Malta while to the right lies Jean de La Valette, hero of the Great Siege and founder of Valletta. Inscribed above his bronze sarcophagus is the following epitaph: 'Here lies La Valette, worthy of eternal honour. Once the scourge of Africa and Asia from whence he expelled the barbarians by his Holy Arms, he is the first to be buried in this, the beloved city which he founded.La Valette's faithful English Secretary, Oliver Starkey, also rests here,the only non-Grandmaster ever to be buried in the Co-Cathedral's crypt.

Above the crypt, reached via the chapel of Provence is the Co-Cathedral's raised altar. Astonishingly ornate, and composed of marble, lapus lazuli and bronze, this is dominated by a single, titular statue in pure white marble of John baptising Jesus. Flanking the altar are two lecturns, one of Moses, the other of an eagle, the symbol of St John, while behind are lined up the choir stalls, all dating from the sixteenth century.

Crossing in front of the altar, one reaches another series of chapels. Part of the first, the Chapel of the Blessed Sacrament, is closed off by a grille through which some of the church treasures that were not looted by the marauding Napoleonic forces in 1798 can be seen; a gate, moulded from solid silver (apparently, this only survived because the Maltese deliberately blackened the gate, so as to make it

The Maltese are masters of lacework

appear worthless), and a priceless icon of the Virgin as Our Lady of Carafa. The keys that hang in the chapel are from three Turkish fortresses that were captured by the Knights in 1601: the fortresses of Mahometta (in modern-day Tunisia), and Lepanto and Passava (both in Greece).

Moving back towards the exit, the next chapel is of Auvergne, dedicated to St Sebastian, and beyond that, the chapel of Aragon, dedicated to St George. Four Grandmasters are buried here beneath monumental tombs, the most notable being that of Nicolas Cotoner. His grandiose statue is supported by two cowering Turkish slaves, proof if any was needed that the Knights carried their hatred of the Turks beyond even the grave. From the succeeding chapel, one can leave the main body of the Co-Cathedral to visit, upstairs, the Cathedral Museum and, downstairs, the Oratory.

The main attraction of the **Cathedral Museum** is its astounding

Door knockers are an increasingly popular purchase

collection of tapestries, all donated by Grandmaster Perellos and all of them depicting religious themes. The other items on display also bear, as one would expect, a spiritual theme: ex voto's, motifs, vestments and so on, as well as a large display of the original scores once used by the choir. An admission fee is charged for this museum. The Oratory was designed as a place of peaceful contemplation for the Knights and it still retains an aura of calm and quiet today. At the far end hangs the huge masterpiece that Caravaggio came to Malta to paint; a superb, chilling portrayal of St John's execution, with much of the background in darkness so as to draw full attention to the terrible act. Note the windows on the right hand side of the Oratory: they are false, painted by Preti to counter-act the real windows opposite and to provide the room with the balance that the Baroque requires.

The final chapel belonged to the combined *langue* of Castile, Leon and Portugal and contains the monument tombs of Grandmasters de Vilhena and de Pinto, rulers who more than most contributed to the profusion of the Baroque architectural style in Malta. The wooden doors of this chapel once opened out into the Oratory.

Back in St John's Square, the street to the left is Merchants Street where a noisy, lively market is held every morning from Monday to Friday. One can buy souvenirs here, but the stalls offer more than the standard tourist fare and for a good many Vallettans, this is the place for the weekly shop. Returning to Republic Street though, and continuing the tour, one encounters in quick succession three busy and cheerful squares.

The first is **Great Siege Square**. This, the smaller and quieter of the three, is marked by a modern, three-figured statue that commemorates the siege, symbolising both the power of the Knights and the fact that the Order's victory saved Europe and the Catholic Church from Ottoman domination. Opposite the statue are Valletta's **Law Courts**, built in the 1960s in tasteful, traditional style to replace the *auberge* of Auvergne, which was smashed by German bombs. There is little else to see here, although immediately south of the Law Courts is St Lucia Street, which will delight those who enjoy shopping for jewellery. Otherwise, continue down Republic Street to the next square, the main centrepoint of the city. This is a wonderful place to sit and sip morning coffee and just watch Valletta go by. Before 1974 it was called Queen's Square. Today, in the new, independent, neutral spirit of Malta, it has a new name: **Republic Square**.

To the right of the square stands, or more accurately sits, the reason for its original name. For here, her imperious features all but concealed by the sun umbrellas of two open-air cafés, and her outstretched arm making a convenient perch for the pigeons of the city, is a statue of Queen Victoria; and behind Britain's longest serving monarch is what is, in a scholarly sense, perhaps the most important building on the island, the *Biblioteca* or **National Library of Malta**.   ✳

The Knights of St John were meticulous in ensuring that their past be recorded in writing. They founded their first library in Malta only twenty-five years after their arrival and, sixty years later, made it law that on the death of a Knight his writings, as well as his property, should revert to the Order. The consequence of this was that within 150 years, the collection of Knight's diaries, minutes of meetings, historical accounts, financial records and so on had grown to such a vast extent that a new library was needed to house them. The Italian architect, Stefano Ittar, was called upon to construct one and the imposing yet graceful edifice that he created is the epitome of scholarly elegance. The library was completed a mere two years before the French occupation thus making it, significantly in view of its contents, one of the final legacies in Malta of the Knights of St John.

Today, the library contains some 300,000 books and manuscripts, many of them housed in the main reading room on the second floor, which is reached via a wide flight of stairs. The bust at the foot of the stairs is of Dun Karm, author of the lyrics of the Maltese National Anthem. Once in the room, the beautifully bound annals of the Knights line the walls but for most visitors, it is the historical documents on display that provide the chief fascination. One can view the original document, dated 15 February 1113, that established the Order, then the Hospitallers of St John of Jerusalem; also the charter, again the original, that granted the Knights the island of Malta for an annual rent of one Maltese falcon per year. The charter is signed by Charles V, King of Spain. In a separate cabinet is a letter to the English *langue* of the Order from King Henry VIII, demanding that they renounce papal supremacy and accept the English Crown as their ultimate authority. This was anathema to the English Knights and they refused their monarchs demand whereupon Henry, never one to ask twice, promptly dissolved the *langue* and confiscated all of its members property and land in England. The portraits that hang high above the bookcases in the reading room are of past librarians.

Yet the *Biblioteca* is as much a living library as it is a museum. Magazine racks stock the latest issues of all the best-known international publications, including *Time*, *Newsweek* and *National Geographic*, and a few lesser-known ones too, such as the English-language *Free China Journal*. This makes the library a fine place to just sit and quietly relax, while catching up on the news.

The last of the three squares is **Palace Square**, the larger of the trio. It is the busiest too, as Republic Street is open to traffic from this point on. The square draws its name from the splendid, two-storeyed structure that fills the right hand side of the square. Now the offices of the Maltese President and once the residence of the British Governor-Generals, it began its existence as the most illustrious of the city's fine edifices and still retains that status today; for this was the **Grandmasters' Palace**.

One of the first buildings to be erected in Valletta, this was designed by Cassar in 1571 for La Valette's successor, Grandmaster del Monte. The palace has changed little over the years, except for a few elaborate additions in the eighteenth century by that most flamboyant of Grandmasters, Pinto de Fonseca. It is through his gate, off Palace Square, that one enters the palace today.

From Pinto's gate, passing a series of plaques that commemorate

The body armour worn by a Knight of St John, Grandmasters' Palace, Valletta

past visits by various members of the British Royal Family, one enters Neptune's Courtyard, which is made shady and leafy by palm and jacaranda trees. Towards the rear is the bronze statue of Neptune himself, trident clasped in hand, that has stood there ever since Grandmaster Alof de Wignacourt moved it there from a position far less esteemed, Valletta's fish market. The Baroque marble fountain behind Neptune was once used to water the palace's horses. In an adjacent courtyard is a clock placed there by Pinto; four hammer-wielding figurines, representing captured Turks, mark the hours.

To the right of Pinto's gate, a plaque chronologically listing the Grandmasters of the Knights marks the beginning of a shallow, spiral staircase that leads up to the second floor. The steps were deliberately built low, so that a man clad in heavy armour could climb them without having to bend his legs unnecessarily. This was a good idea, as even having to stand in a Knight's armour must have been an arduous ordeal. Unlike the Turks, who preferred light and pliable chain mail, the Knights favoured complete body armour and the twenty-four separate steel pieces that comprised a suit would together weigh in at a staggering 49lb (22kg). The Knights would have been trained to fight clad in this manner but by modern standards, such armour appears to be more of a hindrance than a help. Even vision must have been a problem: helmets covered the entire head, with only the narrowest of slits for the eyes to peer through. Several complete suits of armour can be seen lining either side of the corridor that begins to the right at the top of the stairs, appropriately called Armoury Corridor.

Yet along this corridor it is the wall paintings, not the armour, that first arrests the attention. The work of the Italian artist, Nicolo Nasini, the paintings are delicate yet strong in colour and theme, and cover almost entirely the corridors walls and ceiling. As with much of the palace, most of this corridor is sealed off to the public, although one room that leads off it is not. This is the former Council Chamber of the Knights, otherwise known as the Tapestry Room.

This was the seat of the Maltese Parliament up to 1976 and if the people's representatives had ever bored of proceedings, they could at least have gained enjoyment from what hangs on the chambers walls. The tapestries here are huge and wonderfully colourful, and depict some very un-European themes. They date from that great era of exploration, the eighteenth century, and so dwell on the new worlds then being discovered, with images of hunting and path-beating in Africa, Asia and South America. Zebras and elephants peer out from behind exotic plants and semi-naked natives point arrows at their prey. The tapestries became the property of the

Knights by way of a tradition that demanded that upon being elected to their post, new Grandmasters would offer a substantial gift to the Order. These tapestries, and also those that now hang in the St John's Co-Cathedral Museum, were the gift of Grandmaster Perellos. Above the tapestries is a frieze, a masterpiece of intricate detail, that represents the galleys of the Knights doing battle with Turkish ships.

Back at the top of the stairs and directly ahead, is the Entrance Corridor. There are suits of armour here too, as well as portraits of past Grandmasters and more wall paintings by the prolific Nasini. Pinned to the walls are weaponry pieces; staffs, swords and the Knight's round shields. Visitors may enter this corridor, and the Presidential rooms that it adjoins, but only in the company of an official guide. The guides are free, and they wait at the beginning of the corridor until a suitably sizeable crowd has gathered.

The first of the Presidential rooms is the Conference Room which, like the others, manages to combine lavish Baroque with a certain Victorian elegance. A Bohemian crystal chandelier hangs over the large oval table in the centre of the room. Around the length of the walls is a frieze that chronicles the history of the Knights, in superb condition despite never having been restored. On display are Chinese Ming jars, and several portraits of forbidding-looking Grandmasters, including one of La Valette.

From the Conference Room a door opens into the Ambassador's Room, where all of the furniture (the carpets, the curtains, the chairs and the walls) are coloured mauve, creating a rather dizzying effect. The only relief from this solid block of colour is high on the walls, where another frieze continues the story of the Knights of St John. Grandmasters used to receive their most distinguished guests in this room and the President of Malta still does so today; those who have reclined on the chairs in the centre of this room include personages as eminent as the Queen Elizabeth II, the Duke of Edinburgh and Pope John Paul II.

Finally, painted and decorated in yellow, there is the Room of St Michael and St George. Compared to the splendour of the previous two rooms, this is a simple affair, with a wood panelled floor and a plain Presidential throne at the near end. It does, however, boast yet another remarkable frieze, one that reconstructs pictorially each stage of the Great Siege of 1565; the Turkish landing, the battle for Fort St Elmo, and so on up to the final victory. The frieze was painted only ten years after the event itself, meaning that what can be seen here is the most accurate representation possible of what it must actually have been like. At the far end of the room is a minstrel's balcony, supposedly carved out of wood from the same ship that carried Grandmaster de L'Isle Adam from Rhodes to Malta. The balcony is still used by minstrels today, whenever the President feels the need for entertainment on special occasions. The room's exit door leads back out into Entrance Corridor.

Returning to Neptune's Courtyard, a path leads past the god of the sea into what were once the palace stables. These stables are now the home of the **Armoury Museum**, and for those visiting the palace with children this may well be the highlight of the day. The museum is the depository of a marvellous collection of suits of armour and ancient weaponry. One can see pikestaffs, spears, flintlocks, swords, rifles so cumbersome that they had to be supported by tripods, cannons so tiny they look like children's toys. Included in the suits of armour is that which was worn by Grandmaster Wignacourt, or allegedly worn by him, as the suit weighs an incredible 110lb (50kg). The standards that hang from the walls are those of the eight *langues* of the Order.

Back in Palace Square, the elegant, colonnaded building opposite the palace is the Main Guard, once used to house the Grandmaster's bodyguards and later, the guards of the British Governor-General, hence the reason for the Royal coat-of-arms that tops its Victorian doorway. Keeping to the palace side of the square though, and continuing down Republic Street, one will pass a plaque inscribed with the citation of King George VI on his awarding to Malta of the George Cross. It reads: 'To honour her brave people, I award the George Cross to the island fortress of Malta to bear witness to a heroism and devotion that will long be famous in history.' The plaque may well whet the appetite for the **Wartime Experience**, a sight and sound show that tells the story of Malta's resistance during World War II. It is shown in the Hostel de Verdelin, next to the Main Guard. The Maltese are fond of these multi-media shows, with dozens of projectors showing hundreds of slides to the accompaniment of dramatic sound, and the Wartime Experience is particularly good, a stirring, 45-minute account of the islanders courage under horrendous bombardment.

Just off Palace Square, at 59 Republic Street, is an Italian restaurant called the Bacchus which serves good food in a relaxed yet refined atmosphere. It is not cheap, but it often offers 'lunchtime specials' at more attractive prices. The restaurant is a few doors up from the **Casa Rocca Piccola**, once the home of a noble Maltese family and now restored as a private museum. While maybe not being to everyone's taste, the house is a 'must' for anyone with an interest in art, furniture and furnishings as much of that which is on display here is superb.

From the Casa Rocca Piccola there is a choice of routes. There is little of interest along the rest of Republic Street, which from this point on plunges downwards towards the tip of Valletta and the sea. At its end is Fort St Elmo and the excellent **National War Museum**, which is described in Tour Two. Otherwise, one can return to Palace Square and, facing the square, leave Republic Street to turn left into Archibishop's Street.

The first church on Archbishop's Street is Greek-Catholic, the **Church of Our Lady of Damascus**. Inside is an icon that was venerated in Damascus, back in the days when the Crusaders (of which the Order was part) controlled the Levant. As the Knights retreated from the area, first through Greater Syria, later to Rhodes and then around Europe and North Africa to Malta, they took this holy icon with them; now this church seems likely to be its final resting place.

Turn left onto Merchants Street. On the right are two large buildings, both built in the late sixteenth century; the nearer one was once the Jesuit Church, the other once the Jesuit College. The Jesuits did not enjoy good relations with the Knights, and spent much of their time admonishing the Order for their lofty attitudes and excesses. Eventually Grandmaster Pinto tired of them completely. In 1769 he expelled the Jesuits from Malta and confiscated all of their property on the island, converting their college into Valletta University. The building retained that role for exactly 200 years, when the university was shifted to Msida.

Follow Merchants Street down to the junction with Hospital Street, turn right and cross the road. There, signs point the way to the **Malta Experience**, shown in the new Mediterranean Conference Centre, once the *Sacre Infermia* or main hospital of the Knights (described in Tour Two). This is another multi-media, sound and vision show, tracing Maltese history from the neolithic era to the present day and is superbly compiled, enthralling for adults, exciting for children and those with the time or inclination for only one sound and vision shows should make this the one.

The tour ends here. One can either return to Valletta bus terminus (a 15-minute walk, but more fun by *karrozzin* — be sure to agree a price first!) or enjoy a drink and a snack at a bar that is a two-minute stroll from the conference centre. Alternatively, one could follow the steps that lead down from the centre, to arrive at a smooth plateau of white rocks that are gently lapped by the sea and go for a swim in Grand Harbour.

Tour Two • The City Walls

Although it is entitled 'The City Walls', this tour does not unerringly follow those walls. It begins inland, once again at Valletta's bus terminus and moves in an anti-clockwise direction around the city,

The mighty city walls of Valletta

Touring Valletta in vintage style

mostly sticking to the perimeter but occasionally cutting inland where appropriate. It is a circular tour and, along with some wonderful museums and sites, offers superb photographic opportunities en route. There is the chance for a swim in Grand Harbour, too.

From Valletta's bus terminus, cross the concrete walkway over the city's dry ditch and enter Freedom Square through the main gate (for details, see Tour One). Here, before reaching the ruins of the Royal Opera House, turn right. A row of shops is passed — note that the Artisan's Centre is a good place for those last-minute souvenirs, stocking as it does traditional wares from all over the islands — before encountering, on the right, the Fontana Wignacourt. This is an ornamental fountain, the first to be built in the city after the construction in the early seventeenth century of the Wignacourt Aquaduct, which carried water down from the hills near Mdina to Valletta. The Latin inscription above the fountain's façade, *omnibus idem*, means 'the same for everybody', a reference to the fact that everybody needs water, be they a Grandmaster or a humble peasant.

A few steps past the fountain, on the corner of Victory Street, is the barrel-vaulted **Church of Our Lady of the Victory**, the first building erected in the city and designed by Cassar as a thanksgiving for victory in the Great Siege. It cannot be seen but underneath the altar of the church is the first stone that was laid in Valletta, an act ceremoniously performed by Grandmaster La Valette on 28 March 1565. The ornate façade, crowned with a bust of the seventeenth-century Pope Innocent XI, was a later addition.

Across the street, its interior bright under a wide, colourful dome, is another church built by Cassar, this one dedicated to St Catherine of Italy. Little of the architects original work remains, however, as the church was totally redesigned in the seventeenth century. The titular painting above the altar, representing the martyrdom of St Catherine, is particularly fine and is the work of Mattia Preti, creator of the tremendous interior of St John's Co-Cathedral on Republic Street.

The **Church of St Catherine** of Italy belonged to the Italian *langue* whose *auberge*, next to the church at the top of Merchants Street, was built soon after the founding of Valletta. It has since been converted into the city's main post office and the ground floor, where today people buy stamps and send parcels, was once the meeting place of the 'Congregation of the Galleys', a committee comprised of Admirals and leading Captains of the Knights fleet. Their meetings were always held in the Italian *auberge* as, by tradition, the chief Italian Knight would be Commander of the Order's fleet. Opposite this *auberge*-cum-post office is the **Palazzo Parisio**, a discreetly ornamented palace that now serves as the Ministy of Foreign Affairs. It was here that

Napoleon was quartered during his six-day stay on the island in June 1798. At the next junction, where Merchants Street meets Melita Street, is the pretty, circular Church of St James, built in the early seventeenth century and once the property of the *langue* of Castile.

While at this junction, take a look at the stone column there, believed to have once been a whipping post. It would make sense if this is what it was because a few steps away, past St James, is the **Castellania**, which doubled as both the law courts and as the prison of the Knights. Its name arises from the title that was given to the overseer of the Knight's courts, the Castellano, who doubtless would now be suprised at the current function of his workplace — it is the offices of the Ministry of Health. Built in the 1760s, the two Rococo statues fronting its exterior represent the twin figures of Truth and Justice.

To continue the tour from the Castellania, re-trace steps back up Merchants Street to the Church of Our Lady of the Victories. The statue in the square by the corner of the church is of Paul Boffa, the Maltese Prime Minister who oversaw the initial rebuilding of Valletta after World War II.

The entrance to the building that stands only a few paces away from Boffa, on Castile Square at the end of South Street, is guarded by a pair of bronze cannon. This indicates that it is rather a special building. The Maltese seem to have an unwritten, unstated custom of placing cannons, dating from the time of the Knights, at the entrances to the island's most impressive structures. St John's Co-Cathedral has a pair of cannon outside, so does Mdina Cathedral, also the Santa Maria Cathedral in Victoria on the island of Gozo. This particular building so honoured is, however, not a religious edifice. It is the *auberge* of the *langue* of Castile, Leon and Portugal.

This is the most imposing of all the *auberges* of Valletta, built in grandiose yet graceful Baroque. Originally designed by Cassar in his modest, Mannerist style, it was totally remodelled in the eighteenth century on the orders of Grandmaster Pinto, who wanted the *langue* from which he had ascended to be the most illustrious in the city. Many would claim that he succeeded in this, with its entrance adorned with flowing twists of stone, its delicately carved cornices and its overhanging balconies, painted deep green with louvred windows — this is one of the true masterpieces of Vallettan architecture. Unfortunately, it has been claimed by the Maltese government to house the offices of the Prime Minister and consequently, is closed to the public. Another of the Order's buildings, one less impressive, can be seen opposite the *auberge*. This is the squat and square House of Annana, once the Knights administrative centre for the distribution of grain across the island.

Past the House of Annana is a small and pretty garden, replete with two statues. The figure in strident pose, vigorously waving a scroll, is Manuel Dimech, a socialist and early Maltese agitator for independence from Britain. The other is of Gorg Borg Olivier, Prime Minister when Malta was finally granted that independence, in 1964.

A short flight of steps lead up to the charming **Upper Barrakka Gardens**, built by the *langue* of Italy to provide a cool and peaceful retreat for the Knights after the rigours of the day. For the Maltese and for many visitors today, they still serve this purpose, as a blissful bolt-hole of retreat from the hustle and bustle of Valletta, and as the best picnic spot in the city. The roof of the garden's stone arcade has long since collapsed, leaving only bare arches and adding a pleasing touch of antiquity. Several statues appear here and there amongst the trees: of Winston Churchill, and of Lord Strickland, Prime Minister of Malta in the 1920s. Best of all though, is what many consider to be the finest work of the Maltese sculptor Sciortino, *Les Gavroches*, his representation of the hopeless ragamuffins of Victor Hugo's *Les Miserables*.

The views of Grand Harbour from the ramparts of the Upper Barrakka Gardens are stupendous. Far to the left, beyond the immense walls of Valletta, is the entrance to Grand Harbour, sheltered by a breakwater that begins near Fort Ricasoli at the tip of the Kalkara

Grand Harbour, Valletta

promontory. Opposite the gardens, across the waters, are the two peninsulas that form part of the 'three cities': Vittoriosa, occupying the far end of the peninsula and dominated by the imposing bulk of Fort St Angelo; and Senglea, the nearer of the two and home of the dry docks. Behind these two 'cities' is Cospicua, noted for its Cotonera Lines, a great defensive wall that can clearly be discerned. Looking to the right, past the immense silo from which American grain is distributed to much of North Africa, are the shipbuilding yards of Marsa.

From the Upper Barrakka Gardens, retrace steps to the *auberge* of Castile. Once there, turn right into St Paul's Street and follow it past three junctions to find, on the left, the **Church of St Paul's Shipwreck**.

In AD60 the prison ship carrying the evangelist Paul to his trial in

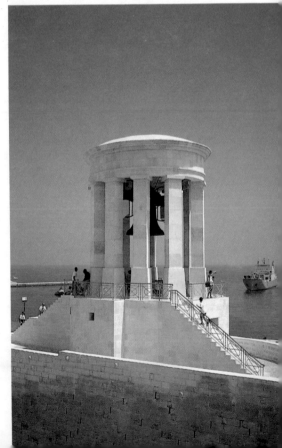

The Santa Maria bell, a modern addition to the historic attractions of Valletta

Rome was shipwrecked on Malta and this church, one of the first to be built in Valletta, is dedicated to the event. Its interior is beautified by intricate wall paintings depicting in detail the life of the saint, although the most striking feature here is the wonderfully ornate Chapel of the Blessed Sacrament, designed by the architect of Mdina Cathedral, Lorenzo Gafa, and dripping with artefacts formed from precious silver and gold. Yet the treasures here are not purely material. There are holy relics too, and what is allegedly an arm bone of Paul is on display, as is, from Rome, a piece of the column on which he was beheaded. The wooden statue of St Paul, designed in Baroque by Melchiorre Gafa, Lorenzo's brother, is quite masterly and is the focal point for the saint's feast day on 10 February, when it is carried out of the church in what is one of the noisiest, most extraordinary processions in the Valletta calendar.

Leaving the Church of St Paul's Shipwreck turn right, go back up St Paul's Street to St John's Street and bear left, going past the Franciscan church and entering a small square. Here there is the Sicilia Bar: with its tables set outside in the shade, this is a nice place to stop for a drink and a snack. From the bar, go past the Grand Harbour Hotel, cross a small walkway over the street below and arrive on St Barbara Bastion Street, which runs atop the bastion of the same name. This is a quiet and pleasant street, lined on one side with old and typically Vallettan buildings that feature the omnipresent balconies, these ones with iron grilles. Looking over the walls to the wharf below, the rectangular hall built by the Knights is now the wholesale outlet for the fishermen of Valletta. Here, every morning, the catch is sorted and sold to shopkeepers and restaurants.

St Barbara Bastion Street curves around to end at Il-Mediteran Street where, at the junction of the two, one can see a brooding and imposing building that serves as the convent for the nuns of the Order of St Ursula. This Order was attached to the Knights of St John and its members still display the Maltese Cross on their robes, its eight points signifying the eight *langues*. There is little chance of seeing any Ursulians though, clad as such: these nuns are cloister nuns, extremely strict, who never venture beyond the confines of the convent. Further along this street is a statue of a lion, its front paws holding de Vilhena's coat-of-arms, suggesting that the buildings in this area were built during that Grandmasters tenure of office.

From here, the **Lower Barrakka Gardens** are a two-minute walk away, gardens that, while being pleasant, are perhaps not as pleasing as their upper counterparts. There are similarities between the two — the arcade, for example, of which only the stone arches remain. They are dominated by an unusual monument, rather like an ancient

Greek temple, that is dedicated to the memory of Sir Alexander Ball, the first and most popular of all the British Civil Commissioners of Malta. These gardens are, however, the best place from which to view one of the newest additions to the attractions of Valletta.

This is the **Malta Siege Memorial**. Opened in May 1992 by Queen ✳ Elizabeth II, it commemorates all those who died during World War II, either in Malta or on the convoys that were sent to relieve the stricken and besieged island. Created by the English sculptor Michael Sandle, the memorial is in two parts. Most noticeable is the bell tower, 15m (50ft) high and containing one of the largest bells ever cast, weighing in at over eleven tons and called the Santa Maria. Next to the tower is the second part, a reposing 6m (20ft) long statue of a corpse, wrapped in a burial shroud. The memorial is grandiose yet sombre, one well suited to Valletta and particularly to its site overlooking Grand Harbour, where the bulk of the casualties were sustained during those terrible years.

The Santa Maria bell takes its name from the story of the Pedestal Convoy, the arrival of which boosted Malta's morale immeasurably during the islands darkest days. The ships of Pedestal left Gibraltar on 10 August 1942, its sailors well aware that their failing to reach Malta would almost certainly result in the islands surrender: Malta had only a few weeks supply of food, fuel and munitions left. The convoy's voyage was short but terrible damage was still wreaked upon it. An aircraft carrier, a destroyer, two cruisers and nine merchant vessels were sunk, but nevertheless those ships that survived managed to reach Grand Harbour to unload 55,000 tons of supplies, enough to sustain the island for a few more, precious months. The tanker *Ohio* epitomised the convoy's struggle. Holed by a torpedo, smashed by a *Stuka* exploding on its deck, it was to limp heroically into Grand Harbour, a destroyer lashed to it on each side in order to keep it afloat. Most significantly for the devoutly Catholic Maltese though, was that Pedestal reached Malta on 15 August, on the feast of Santa Maria or the Assumption of Our Lady, one of the holiest days in the Catholic calendar. So it is that the Santa Maria bell is not just rung every Sunday, but every year on this feast day too.

Leaving the Lower Barrakka Gardens and returning to Il-Mediteran Street, the tour nears the tip of the Valletta promontory. Look out for the steps near the harbour wall: they lead down to a small expanse of white rocks, a nice spot for a dip in Grand Harbour's waters.

The building that dominates this stretch of Il-Mediteran Street is the **Hospital of the Knights of St John**. With all of the fortifications 🏨 that one sees on Malta, it is easy to forget that the Knights were primarily hospitallers who gave as much attention to nursing as to defence. This particular hospital was once the finest in Europe, a place where all who were sick could be treated regardless of wealth, race or religion. Its splendour was legendary: food, for example, was served off silver platters although these platters, like the other treasures of the hospital, were pillaged by French soldiers in 1798. Today the building has been converted into the Mediterranean Conference Centre, and as such has little of interest for the casual visitor, with the exception of the fine sight-and-sound show, the Malta Experience (See Tour One).

Fort St Elmo occupies what is strategically the most vital point on Malta, at the entrance to both Marsamxett and Grand Harbours. The Knights of St John had discovered a small fortress on the site when they first arrived but were quick to realise that it would be inadequate in the face of invasion. They started work on a new fort and by 1552 St Elmo was completed, built to a five-pointed 'star' design. Within thirteen years it was to bear the full brunt of the Turkish attack.

The Turks had moored their fleet at Marsaxlokk to the south of the island, a good bay but one not as sheltered, nor as convenient, as Marsamxett. Consequently, they decided to first berth their ships at Marsamxett before lanching their main assault on the Knight's capital city, Birgu. To achieve this though, they had first to take Fort

Outside the National War Museum, Fort St Elmo

St Elmo, an attack which succeeded but only at a horrible price. What they had estimated would be a four day campaign eventually took thirty-one days, and cost the lives of over 8,000 of their soldiers, many of them the elite Janissaries. Among the Turkish casualties was the aged and feared Dragut, their most experienced commander, mortally wounded by shrapnel.

After the siege Fort St Elmo was rapidly re-built, to the original five-pointed design that had proved so effective. Its walls, however, were never again called upon to withstand a serious assault from land or sea. For centuries, much of Malta's grain reserves were stored beneath it and the lids of granaries — flat, circular stones topped with smaller, flat circular stones — can still be seen in the open space in front of the fort. Today it serves as Malta's Police Academy and so is closed to visitors, except for one section which now houses the

Faith, Hope and Charity

They were old and ramshackle, and hopelessly unsuited to the sky battles of World War II. Even heavily-laden bombers could out-pace their top speed of 250mph (400kph) and at the outbreak of the war, they were not even assembled, just boxed up in crates like giant model aircraft kits. Yet by the end of the conflict, they had written for themselves a glorious chapter in military aviation history. In their own special way, these three decrepit Gloster Sea Gladiator bi-planes epitomised the fierce and stubborn will of the Maltese islanders to resist the German and Italian attacks in any way possible.

Faith, Hope and Charity, as the three aircraft were known, did little to affect the war in the Mediterranean skies. They were too poorly armed and too slow although they were to enjoy some success in downing a handful of German aircraft. Yet their heroism lay in the fact that they were simply there, showing the *Luftwaffe* that they could not have the airspace over Malta totally to themselves: and for weeks they were the only means of air defence available to Malta until several squadrons of Royal Air Force Hurricanes arrived to meet the growing Axis offensive.

During the war, Hope and Charity were destroyed but Faith can still be seen today, minus its wings, in the National War Museum in Valletta. It is perhaps fitting that this was the one Gladiator to survive because, as the Maltese are fond of saying with a double-edged meaning, 'they never lost Faith'.

National War Museum. Of all of the musems of Valletta, two are particularly outstanding. The Museum of Fine Arts, outlined later in this tour, is one; this is the other.

The museum was founded by private enthusiasts in 1974, with the charter of illustrating Malta's role as an island fortress since 1798, the year the Knights of St John departed. The main focus of the museum however, is on Malta's heroic resistance during World War II. There are some fascinating exhibits on display, the larger ones being lined up down the centre of the museum's main hall: the Gloster Gladiator bi-plane *Faith* which, with its companions *Hope* and *Charity*, took on the German and Italian air forces and claimed three kills; an Italian MTB (motor torpedo boat); 'Husky', the jeep used by Eisenhower during his stay on Malta when the invasion of Sicily (Operation Husky) was being planned; German torpedoes, and a clutch of field and anti-aircraft guns. Note the distinctive 'rubble wall' camouflage on the Bofors 40mm gun, a dirty white with irregular black lines that was hoped would blend in with the barren, dry-stone wall strewn, Maltese landscape. Many of the artefacts reached the museum via some unusual routes: the Italian MTB was found in somebody's back garden, the Spitfire engine was fished out of Marsalforn Bay off Gozo and the starboard wing of the Messerschmidt Me-109 came up from the sea bed in a fishing smack's net.

Other exhibits include uniforms and life belts, searchlights and bells, a fine collection of original photographs and an informative display chronicling the withdrawl of the Knights and the subsequent French occupation. Taking pride of place though, is a cabinet containing the George Cross that was awarded to Malta in April 1942, together with King George VI's original, hand-written citation. The museum's official guide book, sold inexpensively at the entrance, features many of the photographs on display and also includes an excellent account of Malta's resistance during World War II.

Exiting the War Museum, turn right. The *auberge* on the left side of the road once belonged to the English *langue* and was kept empty for some 200 years in the hope that the English Knights would one day return to the Order. Finally, in 1784, it was given over to the Bavarian *langue*. Continuing along beside the walls though, one finds oneself atop the mighty fortifications of **St Lazarus's Bastion**, adjacent to Fort St Elmo. The concrete coning tower here was used as a spotting post for anti-aircraft gunners during World War II. It has since been converted into the Gunpost Snack Bar.

At this point Il-Mediteran Street becomes Marsamxett Street, running parallel to the harbour of the same name. The medieval houses here, easily recognisable by their blue louvred window shutters, are the Houses of Catalunya, one-time annexes of the *auberge* of Aragon. Next to the houses, a steep flight of steps marks the beginning of Archbishop's Street. Climb them and enter **Independence Square**.

The domineering, rectangular building to the left of the square is marked '**Ministry of Economic Affairs**', not a title to immediately excite the sight-seer. Pause though, and take a closer look as this is in fact one of the earliest of the *auberges*, the property of the *langue* of Aragon, and built by Cassar soon after the city walls were completed. Since then, it has barely been tampered with at all and has thus, with the exception of its hooded porch, escaped the florid attentions of the Baroque. This means that it is one of the best buildings in Valletta to appreciate Cassar's simple, firm, Mannerist style. Being a government building, it is officially closed to the public but no one seems to mind people popping in for a peek at its sumptuous inner courtyard, ringed with graceful arches.

The *auberge* of Germany once stood opposite the *auberge* of Aragon. This, the smallest of the *auberges*, had fallen into sorry disrepair after the Knights departure and was being used as a bakery when, in 1838, the widow of William IV, Queen Adelaide, visited the island. The queen, a devout woman, was shocked that Malta, a British colony, had no Anglican church and susequently ordered that this crumbling old *auberge* be pulled down and an Anglican church erected in its place. Paying the building costs out of her own pocket, the result three years later was **St Paul's Pro-Cathedral**, designed in foreboding Gothic. The Pro-Cathedral ('Pro' indicating that it acts as the Anglican Cathedral on Malta, yet does not possess full Cathedral status) may not be one of the most architecturally inspiring of Valletta's churches, it is certainly one of the most conspicuous, its 60m (200ft) steeple being a prominent feature on the city's skyline.

The last sight worthy of note in Independence Square is the monument in its centre. This depicts Dun Mikiel Xerri and his companions who, during the French occupation of Valletta when the Napoleonic troops had fled from the outraged Maltese to barricade themselves in the city, had conceived a plan to throw open the city gates and so let their compatriots in. Unfortunately, the plot was found out and the plotters swiftly and publicly executed. The executions took place in Palace Square on Republic Street but this monument was erected here because of its proximity to Dun Mikiel's house, which is at 121 West Street (closed to the public), two doors down from the Carmelite Priory and adjacent to St Paul's. To look up across the street from the house is to see some of the finest examples on show of the wooden, decorative balconies of Valletta.

Turn left up Old Theatre Street for one of the city's largest churches, the Carmelite **Church of Our Lady of Mount Carmel**. The Carmelites have had a church on this site since 1573 but the original was horribly damaged by German bombs. This is its modern day replacement. Its design, a rotunda in overpoweringly grandiose neo-Baroque, has attracted its fair share of criticism but there can be no disputing its sheer impressiveness. There is an almost awesome sense of vastness about its richly gilded interior, an effect heightened by an immense oval dome, one modelled on St Peter's in Rome.

Keep moving up Old Theatre Street, crossing the junction with Old Mint Street, until the old theatre itself is reached. This is the **Manoel Theatre**, built in 1731 by Grandmaster Manoel de Vilhena and, outside Great Britain, the oldest theatre still in use in Europe. Although suffering a long and sorry period of decline — for years it was a cheap cinema — the theatre was magnificently restored in 1960 and it is now easy to appreciate it for what it once was, the focal point of culture for the noblest, most elitist Order that Europe has ever known. The theatre is beautifully decorated, with a green and gold interior design and an exquisitely painted ceiling from which a crystal chandelier hangs. It is small, seating only 600, but in recent

The huge dome of the Church of Our Lady of Mount Carmel on the Vallettan skyline

The defensive ravelin of St Michael's Bastion, Valletta

years has attracted performers of the ilk of Segovia, Yehudi Menuhin and Kiri te Kinawa. For details of performances, consult the brochure published monthly by the *Teatru Manoel* (as it is known), available at hotels and tourist offices.

Turn right after the Manoel Theatre and go up Old Bakery Street which, along with Merchants Street and Republic Street, is one of the main city thoroughfares. Follow it along its entire length to the city walls, passing innumerable shops, cafés and bars. At the junction with South Street, one can perhaps stop for a brief perusal of **St Andrew's Scottish Church**, a nineteenth-century edifice built in typical English Norman style. At the city walls themselves are the offices of the Embassy of the Order of St John. The Knights of St John were reconstituted in 1814 in their original, more humble role of providing relief for the sick and their work still continues today, in the form of institutions such as the St John's Ambulance Brigade. In Malta, the Order administers a large blood bank in Floriana. From their embassy, return to St Andrew's Church and turn left into South Street.

Along here is Valletta's Telemalta office, the place to make international telephone calls or to send telegrams and faxes. Also here are the headquarters of the General Workers Union of Malta, housed in a building constructed out of breeze blocks and cement in the 1960s.

The structure it replaced, the *auberge* of France, was undoubtedly much lovelier but was tragically destroyed by German bombs in 1942. The chief attraction on South Street though, is a sixteenth-century building that once housed the Captain-Generals of the Knight's Fleet and later, the Royal Navy's Commanders of the Fleet, Mediterranean Sector. Today it is the **National Museum of Fine Arts**.

This is a well laid-out, stylish museum and the quality of all that is on show blends harmoniously with the splendour of the building itself, its high ceilings and wide staircases radiating sheer elegance. With three storeys and thirty rooms, there is plenty of space for many remarkable exhibits. It prides itself mainly on its paintings and portraits, the earliest dating back to the fourteenth century and all divided into the school which each is representative of — Florentine, Venetian, Dutch, and so on. The museum's guide book, on sale very cheaply in the foyer, is indispensable as a guide as to the displays, but particular canvases to look out for include the sixteenth-century *Martyrdom of St Agatha*, by Baglione and the seventeenth-century *Allegory of the City of Antwerp*, by Van Thulden. Also the chilling *Beheading of St John* by Stomer and the *Allegory of Malta*, an eighteenth-century work by Francesco de Mura. Two rooms are devoted to the works of Mattia Preti, designer of the interior of St John's Co-Cathedral. His *Baptism of Christ*, exhibited here, is a masterpiece.

The museum though, has more than just paintings. A room is given over to the fine sculptures of Sciortino and another to religious artefacts, such as icons and intricately carved wooden crucifixes. On the first floor of the building a plaque lists past commanders of the Royal Navy's Mediterranean Fleet on which one can espy some famous names; Horatio Nelson, for example, and Earl Mountbatten of Burma. At ground level there is a display of items of traditional Maltese and Italian furniture and in the basement, a collection of various coins of the Knights realms.

Turn right out of the National Museum of Fine Arts. For a drink and a game of snooker, turn right again, down M A Vassalli Street and then into Melita Street to find, at number 111, Valletta's branch of the Royal British Legion. Otherwise, continue down South Street to its end, where there is a small car park. Cross through the car park and you will be atop **St Michael's Bastion** on the city walls. Note the large, flat circular stone on the ground here. It marks the position of a World War II anti-aircraft gun battery. The harbour walls near to it bear the deep and savage pockmarks of shrapnel.

The panorama from St Michael's Bastion is outstanding, a vista of Marsamxett Harbour in its entirety. Far to the right, at the entrance to the harbour, is Fort Tigne on Dragut Point which, with Fort St Elmo, blocks the way in to hostile forces. Next to Dragut Point is the blue waters of Sliema Creek, followed by the next promontory, Manoel Island with Fort Manoel at its tip. Attached to Malta by a man-made causeway, Manoel Island can be explored from Sliema although much of it is best viewed from here. The fort itself, for example, which is now mostly derelict and closed to the public save for a small section that is the base of the Royal Malta Yacht Club. Also the curious arched building, to the south side of the island, called the Lazaretto of San Rocco.

Being a major Mediterranean port, Malta was particularly vulnerable to all sorts of contagious diseases (leprosy, cholera, the plague, etc) which were brought to the island by foreign sailors. The Knights, being hospitallers, were well aware of the dangers of this and so in 1643 established the **Lazzaretto** to guard against this problem, for the Lazaretto of San Rocco was an isolation hospital.

All ships arriving on the island had first to report to the Lazaretto. There the crew would be medically examined and the ships contents and cargo disinfected. If disease was suspected, the ship would then be required to berth in Lazzaretto Creek for a quarantine period of between forty and eighty days; even ships and crew passed as healthy would be quarantined for eighteen days, just in case. Breaking quarantine was a serious offence — death was the penalty. During World War I, the Lazzaretto was used as a more general hospital, as a place where many of those wounded in the Gallipoli campaign were treated, and in 1922, Greek refugees from Smyrna (modern-day Izmir) were processed here in the aftermath of the Greco-Turkish war. Later, during World War II, it served as an administrative centre for the submarines berthed in Lazzaretto Creek. Today, however, it serves no useful purpose and so faces an uncertain future. The promontory to the left of Lazzaretto Creek is Ta'Xbiex, and the creek to its south shelters the yachts moored in Msida Marina. Pieta promontory and Pieta Creek, adjacent to Floriana, complete the vista.

The detached building on St Michael's Bastion is now the office of the Ministry of Justice but was once the House of the Four Winds, so named because its high position left it exposed to the elements on all sides. Beside the house, stone steps lead up to another car park, across from which is the Giannina Ristorante, one of the most exclusive restaurants in the city. Those dining here should ask for a table at a sea-facing window: the views are superb. Turn right though, and enter the **Hastings Gardens**. These gardens could be in better condition — too much concrete and not enough greenery is the most obvious complaint — yet the panorama from the ramparts is

Valletta's harbours are filled with beautiful inlets, this one is Lazzaretto Creek

A magical vista of Manoel Island

another that is truly stupendous. The huge, square base at the entrance to the gardens was once a column erected in honour of the one-time Governor of Malta Sir Frederick Ponsonby, until it came tumbling down in the midst of a lightning storm. The gardens stretch lengthways, along the top of the walls in the direction of city gate and, walking in this direction, one can ascend a ramp to their upper section, which is far better maintained. Half-way up the ramp, one can easily step up on to the thick walls themselves (taking extreme care, of course; it is a long way down) to admire the small, arched bridge that links St Michael's Bastion to the protrusions of St Michael's Ravelin. This ravelin would bear the brunt of any attack, the idea being that if it became at any stage indefensible, its defenders could retreat over the bridge and back to the bastion itself. When all were across they would then destroy the bridge. The statue in the Upper Hastings Gardens is of Lord Hastings, another past Governor of Malta and the man after whom the gardens are named.

Leaving the gardens through the gate near the statue, go down the street opposite to its junction with Ordnance Street and turn right. This leads out into Freedom Square where, on the right, is the very place where this tour began: the city gate of Valletta.

Additional Information

Places to Visit in Valletta

Auberge de Provence/National Museum of Archaeology
Republic Street
☎ 237730
Open: winter, Monday to Saturday 8.15am-5pm. Sundays 8.15am-4.15pm. Summer 7.45am-2pm daily.

National Museum of Fine Arts
South Street
☎ 233034
Open: winter Monday to Saturday 8.15am-5pm. Sundays 8.15am-4.15pm. Summer 7.45am-2pm daily.

National War Museum
Fort St Elmo
☎ 222430
Open: winter, Monday to Saturday 8.15am-5pm. Sundays 8.15am-4.15pm. Summer 7.45am-2pm daily.

Grandmasters' Palace and Armoury
Palace Square
Republic Street
Open: winter, Monday to Saturday 8.15am-5pm. Sundays 8.15am-4.15pm. Summer 7.45am-2pm daily.

St John's Co-Cathedral
St John's Square
Open: 9.30am-1pm and 1.30-5.30pm Monday to Friday. 9.30am-1pm and 3.30-5.30pm Saturday.

St John's Co-Cathedral Museum
St John's Co-Cathedral
St John's Square
☎ 225639
Open: 9.30am-1pm and 1.30-4.30pm Monday to Friday. 9.30am-1pm Saturday.

Wartime Experience
Hostel de Verdelin
Civil Service Sports Club

Palace Square
Showing at: 10, 11am, 12noon, 2, 3
and 4pm Monday to Friday. 10, 11am
and 12noon Saturday.

Malta Experience
Mediterranean Conference Centre
Entrance at bottom of Merchant's
Street
☎ 243776/243840
Showing at: 11am, 12noon, 1, 2, 3
and 4pm Monday to Friday. 11am
and 12noon Saturday.

Casa Rocco Piccola
74 Republic Street
☎ 231796 Open: 9am-1pm daily.

National Library of Malta (Biblioteca)
Republic Street
☎ 236585
Open: 1 October to 15 June 8.15am-
5.45pm Monday to Friday and
8.15am-1.15pm Saturday. 16 June
to 30 September 8.15am-1.15pm
daily. Closed Sundays and public
holidays.

Manoel Theatre
Old Theatre Street
☎ 222618
Open: two guided tours daily, at
11.15am and 12noon.

Hastings Gardens
St Michael's Bastion
Open: 7am-8pm daily.

Artisans Craft Centre
Freedom Square
☎ 246216
Open: 9am-1pm and 3.30-7pm
Monday to Saturday.

Valletta: Useful Information

Tourist Information Centres
1 City Gate Arcade
☎ 227747
Open: Monday to Saturday
8.30am-12.30pm and 1.15-6pm.
Sundays 8.30am-1pm. Public
holidays 8.30am-1pm and 3-6pm.

Ministry of Tourism (not for
    enquiries)
Head Office
280 Republic Street
☎ 224444/5
Open: Monday to Friday 8.30am-
2pm.

Restaurant
The King's Own Restaurant
Republic Street
☎ 230281

Markets
Street Market
Merchant's Street
9am-12.30pm Monday to Friday.
Street Market
Outside city gate
Sunday mornings 9am-12.30pm.

2

THE NORTH-WEST

For first-time visitors to Malta, this tour offers an easy introduction to the island. There is something in it for everyone; from prehistoric ruins to medieval gardens, from fairy tale film sets to golden beaches, from exquisite churches to rumbustious clubs and bars. By circling this section of the island, one can see Malta at its most introspective and rural, and at its most cosmopolitan and frantic. Not particularly demanding, this tour has been designed to take into full account the weather and general tempo of Malta which, broadly speaking, is cool and busy in the morning and hot and sleepy in the afternoon. Consequently, it first travels inland enabling most of the established 'sights' to be seen before lunch, before then heading out to the coast where there are endless opportunities for swimming and sunbathing

Beginning at Valletta's city gate, the tour first explores the suburb of Floriana, which grew up alongside the capital. Suburbia is then swapped for the countryside and the large village of Mosta, which provides an excellent example of the Maltese mania for building mammoth churches. From Mosta, one then cuts west through the island's centre to the prehistoric sites of Skorba and Ta' Hagret, before then moving north to two of the island's finest sandy beaches, Golden Bay and Ghajn Tuffieha. The next port of call is Mellieha, where there is another sandy beach. A delightful excursion from Mellieha, and one not to be missed for those travelling with children, is to Anchor Bay and the *Popeye* film set, used in the making of the 1980 movie in which Robin Williams played the old, spinach-guzzling sea-dog.

The latter half of the tour follows the north coast east back to Valletta. In terms of tourism, this is the most developed part of Malta and in places appears to be just one long row of hotels and holiday

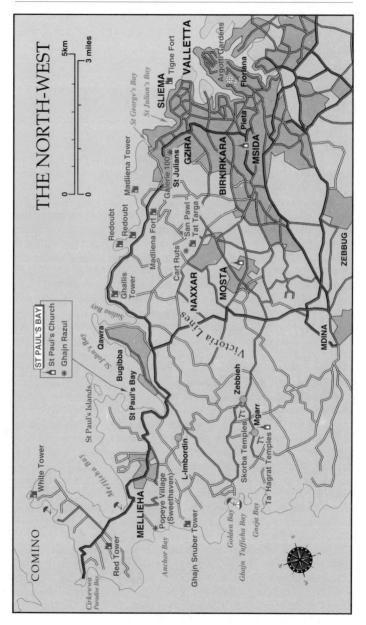

apartments. This may appeal but if not, remember that every cloud has a silver lining and that here are some excellent bars and restaurants, as well as innumerable swimming spots. There is a fair smattering of sights too, particularly around St Paul's Bay, where the great evangelist was shipwrecked in AD60. Nearing the capital, the route passes through the lively seaside suburbs of St Julians and Sliema before rounding the picturesque creeks of Marsamxett Harbour and arriving back at Valletta's city gate.

Those without their own transport will be pleased to learn that this tour can be easily completed by using public transport. Buses are fast and frequent, particularly along the northern coast. There is one exception in that there is, as yet, no bus service to the *Popeye* film set. There are, however, plenty of taxis in Mellieha.

The Tour

Floriana occupies half of the Mount Sciberras peninsula, beginning where Valletta's city walls end and ending where the peninsula begins its protrusion into the sea. This whole area was originally destined to be incorporated into Valletta itself but defence considerations were to deem otherwise: the Knights simply did not have the manpower available to defend what would have been such a large

The fairy tale film set village of Sweethaven, Anchor Bay

capital. Seventy years after the Great Siege however, Grandmaster de Paule directed that the area should after all be fortified and the then Pope Urban VIII, sent his most renowned engineer to supervise the operation and to build the great sea walls of Floriana that still stand today. The engineer was called Paulo Floriani, hence the source of the suburbs name.

Today, Floriana is the commercial heart of Malta and the base for many company headquarters. Ferociously busy, it suffers sorely from traffic congestion, in itself a good reason why the suburb and its associated sights — all of which, ironically, are calm and soothing places — should be explored on foot. Overall, there is not a great deal to see and what there is is concentrated in its centre, only a five-minute walk from Valletta city gate, beyond the bus station and the Triton fountain.

The Knights of St John were well aware that after a hard days praying, working and battle-training, a man's body and soul needs relaxation. For this reason they planted the Maglio Gardens, a thin and enclosed strip of green that stands out against todays concrete surrounds. The garden's name is derived from *Pallo Maglio*, a game vaguely related to lawn tennis that was much enjoyed by the Knights. South of the gardens the flat circular stone slabs that were once the lids of granaries can be seen, as can the Church of St Publius, badly damaged by German bombs but now splendidly restored.

At the end of the Maglio Gardens are the Argotti Gardens, named after the French Knight who planted them, Chevalier Argot. These were the Knight's botanical gardens, where herbs rich in healing properties were grown, and many of the trees that sprout here date back to that era. The gardens are peaceful and cool and today serve a commendable purpose as a government nursery; plants are culti-vated here and then distributed across the island. At the entrance are two interesting structures: a typically elaborate fountain built by Grandmaster Wignacourt, and the circular seventeenth-century Chapel of Surria that was built by Lorenzo Gafa, architect of Mdina Cathedral.

That is it as far as sight-seeing goes in Floriana, save for the seventeenth-century Porte des Bombes, the huge gate at the southern entrance to the suburb that sooner or later, every visitor to Malta passes under. To call the gate beautiful would certainly be an overstatement, but there is no denying its sheer impressiveness.

The immediate surrounds of Valletta/Floriana are heavily devel-oped and densely populated and it is often hard to determine where one suburb ends and another begins. Nevertheless, these suburbs are not short on appeal, particularly those that hug the creeks and bays of Marsamxett Harbour. **Pieta**, the first suburb reached when travelling west out of Floriana, is beautified by its tiny creek and its sixteenth-century Church of Our Lady of Sorrows, while **Msida**, the next suburb on, is quite spectacular. The road curves around the deep blue of its modern marina, filled with both the luxury yachts of the wealthy and the *luzzi* of local fishermen, and passing the striking neo-Baroque Church of St Joseph. This church is typical of how the new Maltese churches have been built to mirror the old, its interior a commixion of the gaudy and the gloomy; brooding religious paintings blend in with the gleaming colour of the altar's canopy, and with the sparkle of stained glass windows set high within multiple domes. A short walk from the church, moored at the Msida quayside, is a rigged schooner called the *Black Pearl*. Originally a private yacht (once owned by Errol Flynn), it was used in the shooting of the film *Popeye* until a terrible storm one night ravaged Anchor Bay and rendered it unsailable. It was then towed to Msida Creek and converted into what is among tourists at least, the most popular restaurant in Msida.

Follow the sea road around through the suburb of Ta' Xbiex, passing alongside Lazzaretto Creek (see Valletta) until a causeway is reached that links Manoel Island (see Valletta) to the mainland. From here, follow the signs to the eminently forgettable suburb of Gzira and from there, the signs out to **Mosta**.

British rule in Malta brought with it peace and stability. Villages that had previously suffered from ferocious raids from corsairs and from the *laissez-faire* attitude of the later Grandmasters, began to prosper and Mosta was one of these. Within two decades, the villages situation had improved enough for the building of a new church to be agreed upon, although opinions differed as to whether the old church should be enlarged or a new one constructed from scratch. To build from anew would mean that Mosta would be church-less while its construction was going on and to the devout villagers, this was a serious problem. However, the architect managed to hit upon a compromise. He would build a circular church around the old, so that services would not be interrupted and only when the new was fully complete, would the old be destroyed; in this way the village gained a new church, without losing a single days worship on the Sabbath.

This church today draws a vast number of visitors because for over 100 years, it boasted the third largest unsupported dome in Europe, with only the domes of St Peter's in Rome and St Paul's in London greater. It would still have that status today had not the residents of Xewkija, on Gozo, decided to go one better and build a church with a dome even bigger. Mostatanians, predictably, brush off any suggestion that they have been out-domed by Gozitans. By their mathematical calculations, they argue, theirs is the greater. But third largest or fourth largest, it does not really matter when one stands inside this marvellous church and gazes up the full 60m (197ft) to the delicately painted ceiling. The dome was built with concentric, overlapping layers of stone, the same technique used by the builders of Malta's prehistoric temples, nearly 4,000 years before. The church's interior is equally impressive; the altar, especially, is captivating, bedecked as it is in silver and with a titular painting depicting the Virgin ascending into heaven. Yet all of this beauty, together with the lives of hundreds of villagers, could so easily have been snatched away from Mosta on the 9 April 1942.

On this day, Allied fighters intercepted a *Luftwaffe* bomber in the

Scuba diving is a popular pastime around the bays and beaches of Malta

skies over Mosta. Following standard procedure, the German pilot immediately jettisoned his entire bomb load, in order to reduce his aircraft's weight and to escape fast. Two of those bombs hit Mosta church. Inside, were over 300 villagers. The first bomb glanced off the façade, knocking off masonry but not exploding. The second passed straight through the dome, landed in the centre aisle and skidded up to the altar. The stunned congregation watched in terror, waiting for it to explode. Astonishingly, it did not. A replica of the bomb can be seen in the sacristy, together with photographs of the damage caused. Maybe the German aircraft had been loaded with defective bombs: or maybe, as the Maltese claim, it was nothing more than a miracle.

A short distance to the north of Mosta, **Naxxar** can claim to be one of the oldest villages on the island. Its name means 'to dry', on the basis that St Paul dried his clothes here after his shipwreck. This is not a story to place too much faith in. Naxxar has an interesting parish church, the seventeenth-century Our Lady of Victory that boasts a feature typical of many of the Baroque churches of the island: two clocks, one a real clock that shows the correct time, the other merely painted. The idea behind this is so that the devil will be confused as to the true time of the church services, and so not be able to trouble

Ghajn Tuffieha beach, curving around the bay

parishioners as they worship inside. Today, many of Naxxar's visitors come here with solely business in mind. For Naxxar is the home of the Fair Grounds, where the Malta International Fair is held annually during the first two weeks of July.

Near the Fair Grounds, towards the north of Naxxar, is the small village of **San Pawl Tat-Targa**, where there are some fine examples of the mysterious prehistoric cart ruts of Malta, etched forever into the rock. Locals will be happy to point them out.

Returning to Mosta and following the signs to Zebbieh, the road descends through the Falka Gap. A geological fault here has caused the landscape to fall away to the south creating a ridge which, at its higher points, bears traces of the Victoria Lines. Although named by the British, these Lines date from long before the British colonialisation, and once specified the area behind which the island could be safely defended from raiding pirates. It is partly for this reason that the north of Malta today is far more heavily populated than the south.

This route runs through a rural, sparsely populated region, one which captures quintessentially the quiet and almost forlorn atmosphere of the two prehistoric sites that lie nearly at the road's end; the temples of Skorba and of Ta' Hagret. These are by no means the most visually impressive of Malta's prehistoric sites and those disappointed in them should not be put off visiting the better-known temples, at sites such as Tarxien and Ggantija. However, for those with a keen interest in how man lived on Malta over 4,000 years before, they are well worth viewing. **Skorba**, near Zebbieh, is the better known of the two. Evidence strongly suggests that this was once a village, the oldest known community on the island, whose residents occupied the site for some 1,000 years, supporting themselves through farming. All that remains for the visitor today though, are the remains of this community's temple, the most obvious feature of which are several tall, free-standing megalithic blocks.

The ruins of the temples of **Ta' Hagret**, reached via the Mgarr road that forks left at Zebbieh, are sparser still. This is perhaps the oldest of the prehistoric sites on Malta and sadly, it shows although the layout of the site can be clearly defined, thanks to renovation work carried out by archaeologists. Most of the original stone blocks used here have since been carried off by generations of islanders, to be used in the building of their own houses.

Mgarr, the only major village on this side of Malta between Mdina/Rabat and Mellieha, is modern and friendly and has little in the way of sights beyond its Church of the Assumption. This edifice is more commonly known as the 'egg church', and not just because of the shape of its unusual, oval dome. It is because during the building of the church, the local priest levied an 'egg tax' on his parishioners; they would give him eggs, he would sell them on at an inflated price, and in this way, money for the building was raised.

The road west of Mgarr descends to the coast through the Gneja Valley, stopping at **Gneja Bay** with its small sandy-pebbly beach. Unfortunately, no bus runs out to this beach so unless you are prepared to walk or to hire a taxi, it is one that will have to be missed. This, however, is no tragic loss as north-west of Mgarr, reached via Zebbieh, are two bathing spots that can only delight.

The beaches of Ghajn Tuffieha and Golden Bay lie in adjacent bays, two great crescents of sand that both effortlessly entice but in very different ways. The smaller of the two, **Ghajn Tuffieha** is almost wild; the hills to its rear are scrubby and sparse, the road that leads down to it just a bumpy dirt track. Tourist development is slight; just a small snack bar to the north. The rocks at the southern end of the beach offer innumerable opportunities for more secluded bathing; indeed, at its very furthest end is Malta's only (and very unofficial!) nudist spot.

Golden Bay beach is only a ten-minute walk away from Ghajn Tuffieha, big and beautiful and overlooked by the Golden Sands Hotel. Tourists are well catered for here; there is a café above the beach and a snack bar on the sand, parasols and sun beds are available for rent and there is a fair selection of water sports on offer, from water-skiing to para-gliding. A tiny part of the beach has been bagged by the Golden Sands Hotel for the exclusive use of its guests. Many people visit this beach in summer and such crowds are a foretaste of what to expect for the rest of this tour, because from this point on, the sleepy villages and hamlets of the interior are left far behind, swapped for the heavily developed bustle of Malta's north-ern coast.

Those with their own transport can reach Mellieha, the next port of call, by turning off the main road and going via the small village of L-Imbordin; those on the bus will first pass through St Paul's Bay (see later in the chapter for further information) and, in all likelihood, have to change buses there.

Mellieha is built above a bay that boasts the longest (although not necessarily the best) sandy beach on Malta. At first, this beach was the town's downfall: the Turkish pirates that once terrorised the Mediterranean found it a highly convenient landing spot and their regular raids led to Mellieha being abandoned in the sixteenth century. British rule, however, proved rejuvenating and the town

One of the tumble-down houses of Sweethaven, Anchor Bay

The Bakers Shop at Sweethaven, Anchor Bay

prospered, initially because of its salt pans — Mellieha means 'the place of salt' — and later, in an historical twist, because of its beach which sees today in spring and summer countless sunbathers. Accordingly, hotels, restaurants and bars abound, as do souvenir shops and travel agencies and all other establishments that constitute a successful tourist town. Yet among the pleasure-seekers that swamp Mellieha are mingled the religiously devout: for in a grotto near the parish church is an icon of the Virgin allegedly painted by the Apostle Luke himself, one that is said to be miraculously endowed with healing powers.

Mellieha's noisy and colourful *festa*, dedicated to the birth of the Madonna, is famous across the island. The evening before the celebrations, crowds gather to participate in the *ghajna*, in which solo singers improvise verses to traditional tunes, each singer seeking to out-do the last.

South of Mellieha Bay (which is sometimes referred to as Ghadira), the road curves over a ridge to descend into lovely **Anchor Bay** and the higgledy-piggledy village that stands on the rocks by its shores. Called Sweethaven, this tatty village, with its steeply angled roofs and tottering chimney pots, seems to owe more to the imagination of

Leaving the ferry from Gozo, at Cirkewwa

Hans Christian Anderson than to the dictates of traditional Mediterranean architecture. It has a single high street, with a bakery and a fishmongers and a blacksmith's forge, as well as a couple of hotels and yet it seems almost too strange to be true; as if, in fact, this was not a real village at all which it is not. Sweethaven is a film set, constructed over a seven-month period and used in the making of the 1980 movie, *Popeye*. The houses and shops have no interiors, the clay roof tiles are of wood, the anchors scattered about are of wood, indeed, everything is made of wood. All sorts of cunning techniques have been employed to make Sweethaven look as 'normal' as possible and it is fun just to wander through, spotting a theatrical con every few yards. Children, especially, will love it. Above the village, a small cinema house screens a slide show that tells the story of Sweethaven but unfortunately, due to international copyright laws, cannot show the film itself. One can, however, buy the video of the film, which stars Robin Williams as Popeye and Shelly Duvall as Olive Oyl, at the souvenir shop adjacent, along with all other sorts of Popeye memorabilia. There is a café here too and, off the rocks of Anchor Bay, the chance for a cooling swim.

Beyond the Mellieha Bay-Sweethaven line is the far western tip of Malta. This is a rarely explored area, primarily because there is so little to see, although it does contain **Cirkewwa**, the ferry port for Gozo, and a handful of relatively uncrowded sandy beaches at the beautifully clear bays of Paradise, Ramla Tal-Bir and Armier, each one guarded by the remains of a redoubt. The tiny fort to the left of the road as one approaches Cirkewwa from Mellieha is called the **Red Tower**, and was built in the seventeenth century by the Knights of St John. Buses run regularly to Cirkewwa, and less frequently to Armier but in all honesty, this is an area best enjoyed by those with their own transport.

Back in Mellieha, head east along the coastal road to **St Paul's Bay**, one of the island's largest bays and rimmed by a solid block of holiday apartments and hotels that curve a full 3 miles (5km) around from Xemkija to Bugibba and Qawra. So clustered are these towns that it is difficult to deduce which one you are in at any given point. All this development may seem surprising when one considers that the bay lacks even the smallest sandy beach yet most visitors seem happy enough, bathing in the sea off the flat rocks off its shores. In other ways, though, the tourist is extremely well catered for, particularly in terms of eating and nightlife: one can eat French at Le Pilier on the Mosta Road, Greek at Yassou at 356 High Street, Indian at the Rojohn on Triq il-Halel, Bugibba, and Italian at the Gran Laguna on the Promenade at Qawra; and amidst this culinary *festa* of international cuisine, one can even go Maltese, at the It-Tokk Restaurant, also on the Promenade in Qawra.

The sight-seer, however, need not feel forgotten. This bay, after all, is where the world's most successful evangelist was shipwrecked in the year AD60. Accordingly, there are several Paulian sites, most notably the Church of St Paul, built on the alleged site where the saint was bitten by a viper yet miraculously suffered no harm. Architecturally, this is an unusual church — a dash of neo-Baroque, a hint of Gothic — with a predictably spectacular interior that includes a seventeenth-century painting depicting the shipwreck. The church has been renovated since World War II; it was badly damaged by bombing, as indeed was the whole area, St Paul's Bay having been used as a base for the great Sunderland flying boats.

West of the church stands the Ghajn Razul, the 'Apostles Fountain' that, depending on who you listen to, marks the site where Paul baptised the first Christian on Malta, or the site at which he took a drink of water. The fountain was deemed suitably holy enough for Grandmaster de Vilhena to build a façade around it, and it is his coat-of-arms that this façade displays.

Looking out to sea from this point, one has a good view of the two islands that stand offshore. They are called, of course, **St Paul's Islands** and their coasts, dotted with underwater caves invariably inhabited by exotic fish, are very popular with scuba divers. For those who prefer a more sedentary form of aquatic exploration, the Captain Morgan travel agency offers trips around the islands in a glass-bottomed boat. The larger of the two islands boasts a domineering statue of Paul, built from white marble on the site where the saint is said to have first waded ashore.

At **Qawra**, the opportunity exists to view more of Malta's prehistoric past although perhaps fittingly, one has to do this while in the grounds of a popular hotel. This hotel is called the Dolmen, after the prehistoric dolmen that it has been built around, a free standing stone formation with a horizontal block supported by two smaller vertical blocks, to create a gateway or window effect.

The next bay, **Salina Bay**, has a rather strong odour which comes from its marsh-like salt pans (*salina* is Italian for salt), located on low-lying plains at the head of the bay where salt is processed in grids by the time-honoured means of evaporation. In past times the area was known as 'the unhealthy plain', the watery swamps being a fertile breeding ground for malaria-bearing mosquitos. Nearby in small and green gardens, the John F Kennedy Memorial Grove is Malta's own tribute to the late US President.

East of Salina Bay, the countryside bears witness to the devastating

Relaxing on the smooth, white rocks of Sliema

Sailing the ocean blue

effect strong winds can have on a landscape. Sparsely inhabited, this part of the coast has borne the full brunt of a north-westerly wind that has blown away top soil and stripped all vegetation save for a few short, spiky tamarisk plants. There are several rocky beaches here that are suitable for bathing, and the odd holiday complex or two, but the most interesting architectural features are the Martello Towers, each one built in sight of the next. These were essentially communication posts, used for spreading news of any attack by corsairs around the island, fast. If a guardsman in a tower spotted the ships of the corsairs, he would light a fire. This would be seen by the guardsman in the next tower who would also light a fire, and so on. It was the Normans who first developed this warning system, and the Knights of St John were quick to pick up on the idea. They strengthened the towers, and fortified them further, which is why many are still in such good condition today. Yet this sense of desolation does not last forever and before long, the skyline once again begins to bristle with buildings as the bays of St George's and St Julians are approached.

This area, along with its sister suburb of Paceville, is another that is devoted almost exclusively to the needs of mass tourism. There is a bewildering selection of international restaurants to choose from, even wider than that on offer at St Paul's Bay, plus boutiques and night clubs and noisy bars and even a casino, open only to tourists and housed in the de luxe Dragonera Hotel. For lovers of art, there is a very good art gallery, Galerie 100, at **St Julians**. Unfortunately, swimming opportunities are somewhat limited, although there is a very small sandy beach at St Julians: to sunbathe here is not quite a case of having your head on the pavement and your feet in the sea, but its not far off.

Sliema, adjoining St Julians, is technically a suburb of Valletta; in reality, it is a town in itself and one with an atmosphere and an importance that rivals the capital itself. Unlike Valletta, which is enclosed within walls, Sliema has had room to sprawl and sprawl it most certainly does, for several miles along its heaving promenade. This is Malta at its most frantic; cars hurtle down the coastal road and people dash about in a way more reminiscent of a London or New York's rush hour than of a small Mediterranean island. During the evening though, all changes as Maltese and tourists alike dress up to saunter up and down the promenade, stopping for a drink at one of the many bars or a snack at the street stalls. There are plenty of more up-market restaurants too; for example, the Bella Italiana Restaurant near the huge Standa department store, which has a good selection of Italian wines, and the Fortizza Restaurant, almost directly opposite, which occupies what was once a coastal fortress. Another fort stands at Dragut Point, at the far northern end of Sliema where the land curves around to almost enclose Marsamxett Harbour. Built in the seventeenth century as the first line of defence for this harbour, the fort is named after Tigne, the French architect who built it.

Even the most ardent lover of Sliema would be hard pushed to call the suburb pretty. Nevertheless, it a place tremendously popular with holidaymakers, and not just because Valletta is only a ten-minute bus ride away. For below the promenade, there is a wide expanse of flat rocks that are ideal for sunbathing and, thanks to short ladders that descend from the rocks into the water, swimming too. Try to exercise some caution while bathing though: the sea can be very choppy and the smooth rocks treacherously slippery when wet. Those with children may want to consider taking them to the far eastern part of the 'beach' where a shallow and enclosed pool has been constructed.

The tour effectively ends at Sliema. To return to the capital, follow the coastal road past Manoel Island and Lazzaretto Creek, and go through the suburbs of Ta' Xbiex, Msida, Pieta and Floriana to arrive, once more, at the city gate of Valletta.

Additional Information

Places to Visit

Floriana
Argotti Gardens
Open: winter 8-11.30am and 1-3.45pm daily. Summer 7.30am-12.30pm daily.

Anchor Bay
Popeye Village (Sweethaven)
☎ 572430
Open: every day except Christmas day. Winter 9am-5pm. Summer 9am-7pm.

St Julians
Galerio 100
100 Lapsi Street
☎ 375907
Open: 10am-12noon and 5-8pm Monday to Friday.

Skorba Temples and Ta' Hagret (Mgarr) Temples
Near Mgarr
☎ 237730 (National Archaeology Museum, Valletta)

3

MDINA AND RABAT

M dina, together with its associated suburb of Rabat, is one of the great joys of Malta. Here the great richness of Maltese history can be appreciated and explored to the full. During the medieval era the city was known as the *Citta Notabile*: 'the noble city'. It is a description that still holds true today.

Mdina was founded some 4,000 years ago, as a fortified Bronze Age settlement atop an easily defensible hill in the centre of the island. It remained as such until the arrival of the progressive Phoenicians, who walled the city and gave it the name *Malet*, or 'the shelter'. Roman rule on Malta saw Mdina, or *Melita* as they called it, consolidate its role as the island's capital and it was here that the Roman Governor would have his residence and his offices. One such Governor was Publius, whom St Paul converted to Christianity during his stay on the island on a spot now in modern Rabat.

The arrival of the Saracens saw the city's name change for the final time. The conquering Arabs were to split the city in two, separating the higher section from the lower and choosing only to fortify the higher, with thick, solid walls and a deep moat. This part of the city they called *Mdina* or 'the walled city'. The lower part became merely *Rabat*, 'the suburb'.

The Norman conquest of Malta saw Mdina retain its role as the island's most eminent city. Its new rulers developed the city further, most notably in their building of churches but as Norman power dwindled a succession of weak and disinterested rulers took ostensible charge. This was a bitter-sweet pill for the Mdinians; on the one hand they were able to arrange their own domestic affairs and indeed took full advantage of this, its noblemen successfully negotiating full autonomy for their city and administering that autonomy through the Universita, a council of leading citizens. On the other

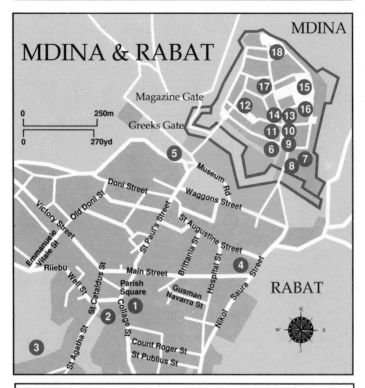

MDINA & RABAT

MDINA

RABAT

Magazine Gate

Greeks Gate

0 — 250m
0 — 270yd

Streets labeled on map: Doni Street, Old Doni St, Victory Street, Emmanuele Vitale St, Riiebu, Well St, St Cataldus St, St Agatha St, Collage St, Main Street, Parish Square, Gusman Navarra St, Count Roger St, St Publius St, St Paul's Street, Britannia St, St Augustine Street, Hospital St, Nikol Saura Street, Waggons Street, Museum Rd

---

RABAT

1 Church of St Paul/St Paul's Grotto
2 St Paul's Catacombs
3 St Agatha's Catacombs
4 Church of St Augustine's
5 Roman Villa and Museum of Roman Antiquities

MDINA

6 Torre dello Stendardo (Police Station)
7 Palazzo Vilhena (Natural History Museum)
8 Mdina Dungeons
9 Chapel of St Agatha
10 Church of St Benedict
11 Casa Inguanez
12 Mdina Experience
13 Casa Testaferrata
14 Casa Viani
15 Mdina Cathedral
16 Cathedral Museum
17 Carmelite Church of the Annunciation
18 Palazzo Falzon/Norman House

---

hand though they had to arrange their own defence of the city, at a time when corsairs were wreaking terrible havoc upon the entire Mediterranean. A raid on the city in 1529 by nearly 20,000 corsairs was only narrowly beaten off.

The following year the Knights of St John arrived on the island. This displeased the nobility of Mdina, who could see their social status tumbling in the face of such an esteemed Order, but they had little alternative but to put up with the newcomers. Besides, the Knights offered a protective shield against the pirates. The Mdina nobles, though, did manage to extract from them a promise that Mdina's autonomy would be respected, an easy concession for the Order who wanted to base their capital at Birgu anyway. Either way though, both sides managed to show their distaste for one another and relations between the Knights and the Maltese gentry were, throughout the entire tenure of the Order on Malta, frosty.

The founding of Valletta as Malta's capital saw a steady slide in Mdina's fortunes. Within decades, the *Citta Notabile* had become the *Citta Vecchia*, 'the old city', as its citizens left for the new wealth to be found in Valletta and Mdina's fine buildings began to crumble into disrepair. Then, almost to add insult to injury, an earthquake in 1693 all but devastated the city. This could have spelt the death knell for Mdina but the city was fortunate that the Grandmaster during this era was de Vilhena, a truly prolific builder who threw himself into restoring the city with gusto. Great edifices were erected, many of which still stand today, and Mdina began to claw back some of its former prestige. In later years it was even to rise in patriotic fervour,

The Church of St Paul, Rabat

for it was here that the revolt began against the French occupation. The British, however, mostly ignored Mdina which suited the still powerful city noblemen perfectly. They retained their power and Mdina drifted on as it still does today, an elegant, lofty city, seemingly lost in the annals of time.

Getting to Mdina/Rabat is easy. All year round there are regular buses from Valletta and in summer only, from St Paul's Bay too.

The Tour

✳ **Rabat** is a town where it is fun to just aimlessly wander. Its narrow and serpentine streets are a delight, particularly those near the walls of the old town, where they display hints of former glory in the most unlikely of places: in the doorknockers, for example, many of which are of solid brass and depict (unusually for a land-locked town) fish, most often the bottlenose dolphin. Stone statues of saints and angels are a regular sight, peering down from their lofty positions at street corners; and many of the windows are traditionally louvred. There are plenty of welcoming bars in this area, ideal stop-off points for a drink and a snack. In the mornings particularly, the town bustles with locals and visitors alike. Nearly 13,000 people live in Rabat, making it one of the largest communities on Malta and although Mdina may have the edge over its suburb in terms of tourist attractions, Rabat is what keeps the area alive.

Nevertheless, there is still a wealth of fine attractions to see. Rabat, after all, was where Paul was entertained by the Roman Governor Publius during the evangelist's unforeseen sojourn on Malta and where he converted Publius to Christianity after healing the Governor's dysentery-stricken father (Acts 28:7-9). On the site of Publius's house now stands the parish **Church of St Paul**, a seventeenth-century edifice built to a cross-plan design that is attractive but by no means spectacular. The altar painting is lovely though, the work of Mattia Preti. Outside the church a raised dias marks the alleged site of where Paul first preached on Malta in a voice loud enough, so it is said, for him to be heard on the island of Gozo. For those arriving by bus in Rabat, this church will probably be the first item on the itinerary; the bus stop is only a short walk away.

Attached to the church is an underground rock chamber where Paul is believed to have lived during his stay on the island. In actuality, this belief owes more to faith and symbolism than it does to historical evidence but nevertheless this chamber, called **St Paul's** ✳ **Grotto**, has been a centre of worship for centuries and a visit by Pope John Paul II in May 1992 served only to further sanctify the site.

Entered by descending a flight of stone steps, the chapel within the grotto is rather incongruously sealed off by an iron grille, through which one can see three statues; Publius, together with his ailing father; Paul himself; and the Apostle Luke, Paul's companion on, and chronicler of, his journey to Rome. Luke was apparently a fine painter and it is for this reason that he is depicted holding an icon of the Virgin Mary. It seems likely that this chapel was at some stage used as a prison; those incarcerated would have been chained to the hooks one can still see in the ceiling.

The grotto itself (St Paul's residence) is open to visitors. It is a small chamber, dominated by a superb marble statue of the saint that was a gift from Grandmaster Pinto. Also here is a lamp of solid silver fashioned in the shape of a Knights galley; along its bows are the eight emblems of the Knight's of St John, one for each *langue*. The lamp was presented to the grotto by the Order of St John in 1960, the year that marked the 1,900th anniversary of Paul's shipwreck on Malta. So holy is this site that for years it was believed that its very walls held miraculous powers; pilgrims would break off chunks, grind them into dust, mix it with water and drink it, in the belief that it was an infallible cure for disease.

If one was able to squeeze through the gap in the rock at the rear of St Paul's Grotto (impossible, incidentally) one would sooner or later come out in another grotto beneath the town. For underneath Rabat is a whole network of catacombs, a network so extensive it seems surprising that the town does not simply collapse into them. Several of these catacombs are now open to the public. They are easy to find, all being on St Agatha Street, a short stroll west of Parish Square and the Church of St Paul. The entrance to the first of these subterranean mazes is immediately on the left as one enters the street and is another site that owes its name to Rabat's most illustrious guest: **St Paul's Catacombs**.   ✳

Why these catacombs have acquired Paul's name is something of a mystery. There is no evidence to suggest that the saint knew of them, or indeed that anyone did up until the year 300, when the people of Roman *Melita* first began to use this interlocking series of chambers as an underground cemetery. This practise eventually died out, as it were, perhaps because there was simply no space left to put the bodies because within these catacombs is tomb upon tomb, of varying styles and variety and all cut out of the limestone rock. Fashioned in the same basic design as the Roman sarcophagi, some are gently arched, others are flat but covered with a rock canopy like a Stone Age four-poster bed; still more are tiny, a sad reflection of the infant mortality rate in those hard, grinding days. The holes smashed in the side of many of the tombs were made by pirates during the Middle Ages in the hope that the deceased's treasures would have been interred with the body: the pirates would have been disappointed. Note the flat, raised, circles of stone that appear occasionally throughout the catacombs: these were what the Greeks called *agape*, 'friendship tables', and the family and friends would gather around them to take holy communion after the funeral. In past times, this cemetery would have lain outside Mdina, burials having been forbidden within the city walls.

At the end of St Agatha Street are **St Agatha's Catacombs**. These catacombs are privately owned by the Missionary Society of St Paul and consist only of a handful of chambers, beautified by fine, vibrantly colourful medieval frescoes. These wall paintings depict St Agatha, who allegedly lived here while hiding from the unwanted attention of the Emperor Decius and who eventually suffered martyrdom rather than violate her chastity with this vicious and lustful Roman. Above ground, the Missionary Society operates a small museum. The museum's upper floor has several examples of Roman and Phoenician figurines but it is the ground floor that is more interesting, a display of relics from prehistoric Malta; sharks teeth, exquisitely detailed fossils and the remains of hippopotami and

St Paul in stone, in the grotto where he is said to have stayed, Rabat

elephants that date back a staggering 175,000 years.

St Agatha Street has a couple of other attractions; the smaller catacombs of St Catalous and a shop called Lacecraft where one can ❋ see the old looms used in forming the intricate designs. If it can be made from lace, you can buy it here although there is also a large selection of knitwear on offer, from bags to jackets.

Return to Parish Square and follow Triq Il-Kibra down to the splendid **Church of St Augustine's**, built by Gerolamo Cassar in 1571 almost as a trial run before beginning work on his masterpiece, St John's Co-Cathedral in Valletta. Cassar's experimentations can be seen in the church's façade, which clearly owes more to the Renaissance than his distinctive Mannerist style. Its huge barrel-vaulted interior, however, clearly found its echo in St John's. A short distance north of St Augustine's Church, Saqqajja Hill begins, where mule and donkey races take place on the afternoon of the *L-imhanarja*, the *festa* of St Peter and St Paul.

Triq Il-Museum (street), which runs alongside the southern walls of Mdina, was cut during the nineteenth century. During the roadworks, the remains of a Roman town house were unearthed and these have since been restored and converted into what is now the **Roman Villa and Museum of Roman Antiquities**. Do not expect to see an actual 'Roman villa' though; very little of the actual house is

Rabat is underpinned with catacombs

left to be seen, with one shining exception; the original mosaics that once decorated the house. These can be found in the basement below the museum in and around what was once the house's courtyard. Indeed it is the mosaic within this courtyard that is perhaps the loveliest of those on display, a geometrical, labyrinthical, three-dimensional design centred with a dove in relief. Other mosaics bear swirling, concentric patterns and a handful are more classically Roman, depicting scenes from the Greek mythology that the Romans adopted as their own: particularly fine is *The Punishment of the Satyr*.

Upstairs in the museum are several other artefacts from Roman *Melita*, such as headless statues and a selection of elephant foot-like capitals. The actual stone that was used was not indigenous to Malta and so must have been imported, showing that the Roman community here must have been a wealthy one. Of particular interest here though, is a display of oil lamps that date from the Carthaginian to the early Christian eras. Note also the small 'tear bottles': mourners would catch their tears in these and bury them with their dead. In terms of 'sights', there is little else to see in Rabat so, from the museum, walk back along Triq Il-Museum, cross over a moat now filled with blossoming lemon trees, and arrive at the main gate of Mdina, the *Citta Notabile*.

❊   With a population of barely 500, **Mdina** is a small city. Its street plan was the design of the Saracens who, unlike the Knights, preferred their cities with narrow and confusingly meandering streets and for good reason. Slender alleyways allow for the easy passage of cooling wind currents through a city; they also offer better shade against the Mediterranean sun. Most importantly, though, they serve the interests of defence well, with attackers having to first orientate themselves before any strategic plan could be implemented. All of which adds to the medieval atmosphere of today's Mdina but makes sight-seeing somewhat problematic: be prepared for plenty of back-tracking.

Mdina's gate is a mere 250 years old. It was built during the reign of Grandmaster de Vilhena, and bears his coat of arms. The interior of the gate portrays the three saints of Mdina in detailed relief: Publius, who, after his conversion, fell from favour with Rome and ended his life in martyrdom in the lion's den; Paul, shown here being bitten by the viper, and Agatha, holding one of the breasts that the Roman Emperor Deicus had ripped from her as part of her brutal murder. Immediately to the left of the gate is the **Torre dello Stendardo** (Standard Tower), now a police station. It too was built during the reign of de Vilhena, as a vantage point for the commander of Mdina's defence forces. This is not the original gate of Mdina. That stands a few metres from this one, but is now bricked up. It was here at this gate that the noblemen of Mdina would greet each new Grandmaster upon his election; the Grandmaster would give a symbolic assurance that the autonomy of Mdina would be respected, whereupon he was presented, equally symbolically, with the keys to the city.

Grandmaster de Vilhena particularly enjoyed Mdina and built his summer palace here, the **Palazzo Vilhena**. It stands to the right of the main gate, a sumptuous affair designed in heavy Baroque and built around a series of shady courtyards. Today, however, its chief appeal is as the home of Mdina's **Natural History Museum**, with various displays attractively laid out within its elegant rooms. This is a rather under-rated museum. The displays, ranging from a geological history of earth to a collection of preserved Mediterranean fish, are thoughtfully and imaginatively presented with education as their forefront aim. There are some fine examples of fossils (look out for the swordfish's sword), and of animal skeletons, including creatures as diverse as the cow and the rattlesnake. There is also a large, and almost unnerving display of glassy-eyed stuffed animals: a cheetah, a monkey, a polecat, even a duck-billed platypus, among others.

Finally, in the immediate vicinity of Mdina gate, there are the **Mdina Dungeons**. Dark and chilling, these dungeons, together with the execution rooms attached to them, lie in the cellars beneath the Vilhena Palace and have been filled with all the grisly implements that were used on the poor souls incarcerated there. Macabre models of wretched prisoners, together with their evil-minded gaolers, peer out from dim corners and anguished cries sporadically split the air.

From the main gate head north into the city, passing on the right the pretty fifteenth-century **Chapel of St Agatha**, which was rebuilt by Lorenzo Gafa after the earthquake of 1693. Nearby is the equally attractive **Church of St Benedict**, which boasts behind its altar one of the fine works of Mattia Preti. At this point though, stop and walk back a few paces to the junction with Inguanez Street. This street is named after the Inguanez clan who were for centuries the foremost family in Mdina and whose descendants still live in the family home, the **Casa Inguanez**, which stands where Inguanez Street meets Villegaignon Street, opposite the Benedictine convent. The nuns of St Benedict have had a presence in Mdina since the fifteenth century and today's Sisters still live by the same zealously strict laws that their forebears did: for example, never being allowed to venture outside of the convent. It is virtually impossible to visit the convent (totally impossible, if you are male) but its very presence here only serves to add to the timeless aura of this ancient city.

A stroll along the length of Inguanez Street further reinforces this aura. The street hugs the fortified southern wall of Mdina, and into this wall over the centuries a variey of workshops and storehouses have been built, many of which are still in use today. The Saracen influence in the architecture is strong, most notably in the pointed arches (resembling a bishop's mitre) rather than the rounded arches favoured by the Normans and the Knights. In a vault beneath the walls along this street, what was once a musketry and power room is now the atmospheric Bacchus Restaurant, with fine food to match its stylish surroundings.

✳   At the end of Inguanez Street is **Greeks Gate**, named after the Greek community that once thrived here. When the Knights of St John were expelled from Rhodes many of the indigenous Rhodians were reluctant to be left at the mercy of the often merciless Turks, and so sailed with the Knights. A sizeable proportion of them settled in

The long approach to De Vilhena's Gate, Mdina

this part of Mdina, thus giving this gate, which was later re-modelled in Baroque, its name. Take a close look at the wall adjacent to the gate, and note that some of the bricks are older than others; the site of the new bricks shows those areas of the walls that corsairs breached in their raids on the city. Further evidence of violence can be seen in the area in the pock-marked walls of some of the houses, particularly on the house opposite the gate at the junction with St Nicholas Street; the pock-marks almost certainly came from lead musket balls fired in the uprising against the French at the end of the eighteenth century.

From Greeks Gate, follow the walls around to the west along Magazine Street, where many of the buildings were once used as armouries. Along here is Mdina's third gate, **Magazine Gate**, opened ✳ in the nineteenth century as the entrance for those arriving in Mdina on the train from Valletta. With its commanding vista over the lush valley

Lorenzo Gafa's masterpiece, St Paul's Cathedral, Mdina

of Mtarfa below, the view from here is lovely. This gate, however, is no longer in use, the railway line having been closed in 1932.

Leave Magazine Street at St Peter's Street. There is a nice example of Norman architecture here, in the dual-arched windows of the house that stands at the junction of the two. Go down St Peter's Street, turn right into St Nicholas Street and follow it to its end, at St Nicholas's Chapel. Turn right again and enter **Mesquita Square**, named after the Spanish commander of the forces in Mdina during the Great Siege. It is in a beautiful, immaculately maintained old house off this square that one can view the **Mdina Experience**, a dramatic, forty-five minute show that relates the rich history of the city in pictures and music.

Head west from Mesquita Square, down Mesquita Street to where it joins the main thoroughfare of Mdina, Villegaignon Street. Here there is the crested façade and red doors of the **Casa Testaferrata**, family home of another noble family of Mdina, and opposite it, the **Casa Viani**, from whose balcony the French commander was thrown at the beginning of the revolt against the hated French occupation. Or so it is said; there is, unfortunately, little historical evidence to back up the claim that this was the actual house. Just beyond the Casa Testaferrata are Mdina's municipal government offices, housed in a grand old building. Matters of great local importance have been discussed here for centuries because it was here, in what is called the Banca Giuratale, that the *Universita*, the committee of noblemen that governed Mdina in the days before the Knights, would meet to deliberate.

Immediately beyond these government offices is the centre of Mdina, **St Paul's Square**. There are several fine buildings bordering this square but there is one that outshines all others in size, stature and in sheer magnificence: one of the great masterpieces of Lorenzo Gafa, **Mdina Cathedral**.

This cathedral marks the spot on which Paul converted the Roman Governor Publius to Christianity yet it was not until around the year 1100 that a suitably impressive church was built here. It was constructed on the orders of the Norman, Roger, and stood for some 600 years until the earthquake of 1693 devastated the city, and the church with it. Accordingly, the devout Knights, who found it an anathema that such a holy site should have no church, despatched the architect Lorenzo Gafa to Mdina with instructions to build anew, in the Baroque style of the day. Gafa threw himself into the task and the result is, notwithstanding one or two later additions such as the stained glass windows, much as it can be seen today.

The exterior of this cross-planned church is painstakingly proportioned, the façade ornate without being gaudy. Two clocks either side of the entrance reaffirm this fine balance, one clock telling the time, the other the day and the month. There are two bronze cannons too, both dating back to the days of the Knights. Yet as with so many of the great Baroque churches of Malta though, it is the interior that takes the breath away.

Initially, comparisons with St John's Co-Cathedral in Valletta are hard to avoid. There is that same sense of great richness, in the huge paintings and chandeliers, in the awesome sense of vastness beneath its brilliantly painted barrel-vaulted ceiling, in the colourful spangle of tombstones that make up the floor, the bones of priests and Knights resting below them. Yet this cathedral seems to be imbued with a calmness, a serenity that St John's does not quite attain. The paintings are dark, almost restful — even the titular painting depicting the shipwreck of St Paul carries a sense of calm. It is here at the altar that some of the finest treasures of the cathedral can be seen, beneath and around the gilt-edged canopy where, to preserve the balance, there is a pair of everything; two magnificent organs, two oval mosaics and two statues-cum-lecturns, the one on the right facing the altar being St Luke, the other St John. To the left of the altar, there is the small Chapel of the Blessed Sacrament, centred with a Byzantine-style icon of the Virgin Mary, another that is reputedly the work of the painter-cum-apostle St Luke. Directly opposite this chapel there is a particularly fine wall painting, a symbolic representation of St Paul driving the Turks away from the walls of Mdina. Also near the altar is a silver processional cross, which was brought by the Knights from Rhodes.

Gafa's love of the heavy Baroque permeates nearly every aspect of St Paul's and although much of his work was, in effect, a re-building job, this is still very much his church. Indeed, for many observers this cathedral marks the pinnacle of his career. As for what remains of St Paul's that predates the 1693 earthquake, there is very little. However, the Norman-style font near the entrance is original, as are the vestry doors at the side of the cathedral. These were once the main entrance doors, fashioned from solid Irish oak and were presumably considered far too good to merely discard.

Adjacent to St Paul's Cathedral is the **Cathedral Museum**, which is a cut above other museums on Malta of a similar ilk. Here one can view much of what was salvaged from the pre-1693 church, including Papal Bulls and immaculately illuminated Norman choirbooks that date back to the eleventh century. There is a fine coin collection too, as well as paintings, artefacts from the Roman era in Mdina and, best of all, a display of marvellous woodcuts by the sixteenth-century artist Albrecht Dürer, prints of which can be bought in the museum shop. The museum is housed in the old Archbishop's Seminary, which was built on the foundations of a Roman villa where the famous second-century statesman and orator Cicero, once stayed.

Returning to, and continuing down, Villegaignon Street one soon encounters the **Palazzo Santa Sofia**, an unusual building with a ground floor in plain, Norman style and a first floor in Baroque. Across the street from this palace is The Maltese Falcon, one of those useful shops that seems to sell every type of Maltese souvenir available, thus making it a good place for last minute shopping; and further down still is the **Carmelite Church of the Annunciation**, an early seventeenth-century edifice and the site where the revolt against the hated French first exploded, when the occupiers began to auction off the church treasures. Finally, as Villegaignon Street draws to an end, there is the **Palazzo Falzon**, the Norman House, built in the sixteenth century and one of the oldest surviving buildings of this ancient city. This is said to have been the first residence of Grandmaster de l'Isle Adam upon his arrival in Malta.

It is at **Bastion Square**, at the end of Villegaignon Street, that the one-time strategic importance of Mdina is fully revealed. This is one of the highest spots on Malta and, from the ramparts here, one can see as far as St Paul's Bay. Dominating the skyline though is the huge dome of the church at Mosta. This is a lovely viewing spot and perhaps one best appreciated from the Fontanella Tea Garden,

Mdina's narrow and atmospheric streets

which enjoys a fine reputation for its chocolate cakes. There is another fine vista to be enjoyed at another bastion, De Redin's, which lies behind the cathedral and which can be easily reached from Bastion Square simply by walking east up Bastion Street.

From here, walk south down St Paul's Street past the Xara Hotel, an old converted mansion and one of the few places to stay in the city. The elaborate balcony on the building opposite the hotel is the Herald's Loggia, from where a herald would announce the Grandmaster's edicts to Mdina's populace. Turn right at this point and the main gate of Mdina, and the end of the tour of this *Citta Notabile*, is only a few paces away.

Additional Information

Places To Visit

MDINA

Mdina Dungeons
St Publius Square
☎ 450267
Open: October to May 10am-6pm. June to September 10am-7pm.

Mdina Experience
7 Mesquita Square
☎ 454322/450055
Showing: 11am, 12noon, 1, 2, 3 and 4pm Monday to Friday 11am, 12noon, 1pm Saturday. Closed Sunday.

Mdina Cathedral
St Paul's Square
Open: 9.30-11.45am and 2-5pm daily.

Cathedral Museum
St Paul's Square
Open: 1 October to 31 May 9am-1pm and 1.30-5pm Monday to Saturday. June to September 1.30-5pm Monday to Saturday. Closed Sundays and public holidays.

Natural History Museum
Vilhena Palace
St Publius Square
☎ 455951 Open: winter 8.15am-5pm Monday to Saturday and 8.15am-

4.15pm Sunday. Summer 7.45am-2pm daily.

Bacchus Restaurant
Inguanez Street
☎ 454981

RABAT

Roman Villa and Museum of Roman Antiquities Esplanade
☎ 454125 Open: winter, 8.15am-5pm Monday to Saturday and 8.15am-4.15pm Sunday. Summer 7.45am-2pm daily.

St Paul's Catacombs
St Agatha Street
Open: winter 8.15am-5pm Monday to Saturday and 8.15am-4.15pm Sunday. Summer 7.45am-2pm daily.

St Agatha's Catacombs
St Agatha Street
Open: 9-11.45am and 1-4pm Monday to Saturday. Closed Sundays and public holidays.

Lacecraft
20a St Agatha Street
Rabat
☎ 454311
Open: 9am-5pm Monday to Saturday.

4

CENTRAL MALTA

Getting off the beaten track can sometimes pose a problem on Malta. The island is small and extremely popular and at times, particularly in the height of summer, it can be hard to escape the press of fellow itinerants. This tour however, a circular sweep through the island's centre, attempts to do just that, eschewing many of the more conventional 'sights' in favour of a Malta that is quieter, calmer and in certain places, staggeringly beautiful. This is not to say that there is little to actually 'see' on the tour: indeed, it manages to touch upon some remarkable spots, ranging from the relics of prehistoric man to luscious gardens built by aristocratic Grandmasters; and for the sake of some relief, it also visits several sites that are very much on the standard tourist track.

The tour starts at the island's main bus station, at Valletta's city gate, and passes through the suburbs of Floriana and Hamrun before arriving at the 'three villages' of Lija, Attard and Balzan, where medieval Malta mingles with the modern. Mdina and Rabat (covered separately in Chapter 3) is the next stop and although these two fine towns really deserve a full day in themselves, those short of time can include them on this tour. Then one moves south again, past the village of Dingli to the southern coast and spectacular scenery and some intriguing examples of that very Maltese prehistoric oddity, 'cart ruts'. Following the tour from here, the prehistoric temples of Hagar Qim and Mnajdra can be explored before reaching the Blue Grotto, where one can bathe in a sea of magical blue before turning north on the return leg to Valletta.

To complete this tour by public transport alone is an impossible task. The first section of the tour is easy enough: buses run very regularly between Valletta, the 'three villages' (all three are sited close enough together to make walking no problem at all) and

Mdina/Rabat. Note, however, that some buses from Valletta to the 'three villages' do not go via Hamrun.

There is also a more limited service from Rabat to Dingli. From this point on though, one's own transport is a necessity.

The Tour

From Valletta's city gate, one can begin this tour either by a walking tour of Floriana (Chapter 2) or by travelling immediately south, through **Hamrun** which is second only to Sliema as Valletta's largest suburb. Hamrun, however, has little of Sliema's appealing bustle and consists mainly of one long and rather dreary high street with smaller residential streets leading off it. Nevertheless, it offers the chance of a glimpse into Maltese suburbia and a pleasant half-hour can be spent wandering up and down the street, poking around the shops and bars and visiting the huge parish church of San Gejtanu, carefully crafted in neo-Baroque and visually stunning in the way most Maltese churches are. The church is the focal point for Hamrun's spectacular *festa*, an event not to be missed by anyone who is in Malta during the second week of August.

South-west of Hamrun en route to the 'three villages' of Lija, Attard and Balzan is the suburb of **Santa Venera** where the Casa Leoni, a startlingly ornate house built in the early eighteenth century, can be seen, as well as what remains of the Wignacourt Aquaduct, built by the Grandmaster of the same name to carry water down from Mdina to Valletta. The aquaduct stands on the edge of the three villages but before visiting these villages, one may want to consider a detour due south of Hamrun, to the adjacent suburb of **Qormi**.

This is an old town, established in 1436 and with a twisting, medieval street lay-out that dates back to its very inception. It is renowned for its fine examples of medieval architecture that can be seen in its balconies and windows but most notably in the now rather delapidated Stagno Palace, built in the sixteenth century and with a façade that displays a multitude of styles. Towards the east of the suburb is the parish Church of St George, built by an unknown architect in the sixteenth century who was clearly a master of his art. The church is tall and rigidly precise, each aspect of detail carefully attended to, like a soldier on parade in full dress uniform. The chapels of St Catherine, St Mary and St Peter are clustered together in the centre of Qormi, the former dating from the seventeenth century, the latter two from the sixteenth. Qormi has a reputation as the bread-making centre of Malta and was originally known as the *Casal Fornaro*, 'the Bakers Village'.

In recent years the 'three villages', Lija, Attard and Balzan, have

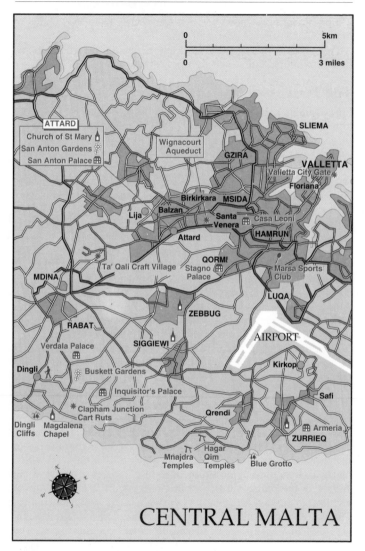

| 0 | | | | | | 5km |
| 0 | | | | | | 3 miles |

ATTARD
Church of St Mary
San Anton Gardens
San Anton Palace

Wignacourt
Aqueduct

SLIEMA

GZIRA

VALLETTA
Valletta City Gate
Floriana

Birkirkara   **MSIDA**

Lija   **Balzan**
Santa   Casa Leoni
Venera
HAMRUN
Attard

QORMI
Ta' Qali Craft Village   Stagno   **Marsa Sports
Palace   Club**

MDINA

LUQA

ZEBBUG

RABAT

SIGGIEWI   **AIRPORT**
Verdala Palace

Kirkop
Dingli   Buskett Gardens

Inquisitor's Palace

Safi

Clapham Junction
Cart Ruts
Dingli   Qrendi
Cliffs   Magdalena
Chapel   Armeria
ZURRIEQ

Hagar
Mnajdra   Qim   Blue Grotto
Temples   Temples

CENTRAL MALTA

undergone something of a renaissance. These one-time medieval
settlements are now firmly in vogue among the well-heeled of Malta
and on the outskirts of Attard in particular, the streets are lined with
graceful modern villas, all with immaculately tended gardens. The
villages (or more accurately, towns as their combined population is

The Baroque façade of San Gejtanu Church, Hamrun

Hamrun high street, decorated for the spectacular festa

now nearly 11,000) new found wealth though, can in no way disguise their origins; the centre of each is a spiders web of intricate, narrow, pavement-less streets, designed in the Arabist pattern and bordered by sixteenth- to eighteenth-century houses that bear all the distinctive hallmarks of traditional Maltese architecture; ornately carved façades, religious emblems and louvred windows, shuttered with a latticed grille so that those inside can look out, but those outside cannot look in.

The 'three villages' all have their own parish church and while each church is essentially similar — all retain the original Latin cross-plan design with a narrow façade and no side aisles — each one also has its own unique appeal. For example, Lija's Church of Christ the Saviour is built in a curious combination of Gothic and Baroque, with an almost Byzantine octagonal dome. Behind the altar within its colourfully be-frescoed interior, a titular statue depicts the Trans-figuration. This church was completed in 1694, one year before work ended on the equally pretty Church of the Annunciation in Balzan.

Those with time for only one church though, should make it the Church of St Mary in **Attard**. Designed by its twenty-two-year-old architect Dingli, this shows little adherence to any one style. Instead it is an utter conglomoration; ostensibly Baroque, but with a heavy splash of the Renaissance and more than a hint of the Corinthian. Its shallow octagonal dome is part of the original 1613 church, but the belfry was added 100 years later and the clock 150 years after that. The barrel-vaulted interior gives off a much larger impression of size and space than the almost modestly-sized exterior would suggest. All told, this church is a splendid example of the richness in religious architecture that the Knights of St John brought to Malta. Yet of course, this was not all that the Knights brought to the island, and to Attard.

The Knight's of St John were at first grieviously disappointed with Malta. It was far too barren, much too arid for this cultured Order, whose previous home had been the beautiful Greek island of Rhodes. To compensate for this, they busied themselves planting lush gardens, one of which can be seen on the outskirts of Attard opposite the five-star Corinthian Palace Hotel, where the village borders Lija and Balzan; these are the San Anton Gardens, which incorporate within their surrounds, the grand **San Anton Palace**.

The palace was built first in 1620 by Antoine de Paule, a man who two years later was to become Grandmaster de Pauleand so moved to Valletta. He kept the palace though, as a summer retreat, and since then it has been in almost continual use. It was the seat of the Maltese National Assembly after the revolt against the French in 1799; it was the British Governor-General's summer residence up to 1928 and after that, his permanent residence; and today it is the home of the President of Malta. Because of this, much of the palace is sealed off to visitors. Nevertheless, the gardens are open to all, and very charming they are too. Trees and plants have been brought in from across the world — for example jacarandas from South America, eucalyptus from Australia — and the original aim of the Knights, to create a gaily colourful oasis within the dull browns of the Maltese landscape, is still amply fulfilled today. There is a pond for swans and geese, a Baroque fountain and, in the heart of the gardens, a small zoo with Libyan *whadden* (goats), camels, monkeys, pheasants and cranes. It is said that the landscape gardener who designed the San Anton was also responsible for the huge and gorgeous gardens at the Palace of Versailles, just outside Paris, and indeed both follow the same plan. This theory is by no means inconceivable — the Knights were never content to employ only the second-best.

From the 'three villages', the road climbs steadily upward through some of Malta's most fertile countryside to Rabat and its citadel of Mdina. There is little to see en route, although shoppers may wish to stop off at the Ta Qali Crafts Village, housed in an old aerodrome dating from World War II, where the full range of Maltese souvenirs are on show and for sale. At this point, one can either tour Mdina and Rabat (see Chapter 3) or save them for another day. Those deciding upon the latter should head south from Rabat, climbing steadily up a road bordered with fertile fields, to **Dingli**. Situated 250m (820ft) above sea level, this is the highest village on Malta and although it possesses little of interest in itself, the walks to be had in its vicinity are wonderful. Best is the walk (or drive) south to the edge of the Dingli Cliffs where Malta, quite literally, appears to fall into the sea.

One owes the beautiful vista from the **Dingli Cliffs** to a tremendous earthquake that shattered this region millions of years ago. Its tremors rocked Malta so badly that the entire southern part of the island collapsed, leaving only the tiny islet of Filfla as evidence that it ever existed. The cliff face, however, is not sheer nor is it entirely rocky. Instead, it rolls downwards at an angle gentle enough to allow farmers to cultivate it. Lucky is the farmer who has rights to grow crops on the side of the Dingli Cliffs; this is one of the few parts of Malta that is completely protected, by the higher land behind, from the destructive north-westerly wind.

On the edge of the Dingli Cliffs the tiny and disused chapel of St Magdalena can be seen. In travelling rural Malta, one will see several of these forlorn chapels, often built in the middle of nowhere in particular. Most were built in the last two centuries, usually by rich families who had received a blessing from above, such as a cure from a terrible sickness, or the birth of a son. In time though, they fell into disrepair and ended up being used by only one section of society — criminals who, when on the run, would flee to the chapels and piously claim religious sanctuary. Eventually, the church authorities tired of being constantly put in this somewhat invidious position. The chapels were ecclesiastically deemed not to be places of sanctuary and inscribed tablets were placed above the door of most of them, declaring this to be so.

From the cliffs, return to Dingli and take the north-eastern road to the **Verdala Palace**. This is the Chequers or Camp David of Malta, the place where the Maltese President entertains esteemed guests, but its history easily predates its British and American counterparts. Resembling more of a castle than a palace, it was built in 1586 by Grandmaster de Verdalle as a summer home over the site of Grandmaster de la Valette's hunting lodge (tradition relates that Valette

The panorama from the Dingli Cliffs is breathtaking

died of a heart attack brought on by a particularly vigorous days hunting here) to a design drawn up by Valetta's most prolific architect, Gerolamo Cassar. Verdalle was not a man over-given to modesty, and the palace's Great Hall is lined with wall paintings depicting great moments in his life.

One of the most pleasing aspects of the Verdala Palace is its surrounds. Generally speaking, trees are in short supply on Malta but here, in what has become known as the Buskett Gardens, there are enough to constitute if not exactly a forest, then at least something more than a copse. In fact, *buskett*, a word drawn from the Italian *boschetto* or 'little wood', sums them up perfectly. Originally planted by the Knights as a place in which to rear their hunting falcons, the gardens are shady and filled with sweet-smelling firs, and are very popular amongst Maltese picnickers. They are even more popular during the most splendiforous *festa* on the island's calendar,

*Cart ruts; a prehistoric
Maltese mystery*

Cart Ruts

They appear all over Malta and Gozo: great grooves scratched deeply into the rocky landscape, often knee-deep and equally wide, some located on plateaux inland, others mysteriously disappearing over the edge of sheer cliffs at the coast. For centuries people were baffled as to what they were; their existence was even, according to the beliefs of an imaginative few, put down to the presence of extra-terrestial beings. Thanks to the efforts of brilliant archaeologists, these grooves can, in part, be explained.

In the days of prehistoric Malta, man had had to have a way of transporting his produce and his building materials from A to B. Without wheels, this would have been difficult. Yet prehistoric man was nothing if not ingenious. He had draught animals, such as oxen, and he yoked these beasts to plough-type wooden shafts, the ends of which would drag along the ground behind the animal. He could then put crossbars between these shafts, balance his loads on them, and go. Unfortunately, the rocky surface of Malta would have worn the tips of these shafts away and so to prevent this, he attached stone blocks to them, thus reducing wear and tear on the precious wood. Over the years, as these primitive carts ('slide-cars', as they are now known) worked their way across the island, they wore ruts into the surface. Prehistoric man would not have been

Limanarja. This *festa*, the 'festival of light', is held on the feast day of St Peter and St Paul (29 June) and celebrates the end of harvest time. On the eve of the great day, participants walk in their hundreds from Mdina to these gardens and settle down for a night of country music and singing, merrymaking and drinking and eating the traditional dish of *Limanarja* (fried rabbit). Revellers often stay overnight in the gardens, sleeping under the trees, and there is no reason why hardy visitors to the island should not do likewise.

Leaving the Buskett Gardens, take the left (south) road, round a hill and head up a dirt track marked 'private' (don't worry about this). From here, a plethora of prehistoric cart ruts are a ten-minute walk away. Cart ruts can be seen all over Malta and although it may seem blasé to state that if you have seen one, you have seen them all, it is nevertheless true. However, you *must* see one example and these, the 'Clapham Junction' cart ruts are amongst the most remarkable. It may seem odd to name a prehistoric site after Europe's busiest railway station but when one views this astonishing collection of interlocking grooves, some of them having scored creases knee-deep aware of these ruts: Malta had a good deal more top soil then than it does today and the soil would have formed a crust over the grooves. As centuries passed though, the top soil was blown away thus revealing to all the 'cart ruts' of Malta.

All of which is very plausible and highly likely. Yet it does not explain one mysterious factor. The carts would have had to be pulled by something, be that a draught animal or man, and the passage of the 'puller' would also have surely marked the landscape, somewhere between the parallel cart ruts. Yet marks of this type are nowhere to be found and as to why not, no one can be sure.

The cart ruts represent paths from one settlement to another and, what was good for a path in 2000BC is often good enough in AD2000, these paths often parallel modern roads. The reason for some of these ancient roads disappearing over the edge of cliffs can be easily explained: the land at these points, has simply fallen into the sea, leaving only the deep grooves as evidence that a settlement once existed at a point where today one can see only ocean.

To best view the cart ruts, go to either San Pawl Tat-Targa, near Naxxar; to 'Clapham Junction' (named thus because the grooves are so numerous and inter-connecting) south of the Buskett Gardens; to Borg-in-Nadur, near Ghar Dalam and Marsaxlokk, or to an enclosure near the grounds of the hospital near Mtarfa, west of Mdina. On Gozo, they can be seen near the cliffs at Ta'Cenc.

and a car tyre wide, it is easy to see why.

From Clapham Junction, follow the road around to the cliffs and then head north on the road to Zebbug. This route passes the seventeenth-century **Inquisitor's Palace**, set in lovely gardens. The palace was used by the Inquisition as a summer residence during those periods when they descended upon Malta to wreak fear and terror among its people. According to folklore, the Inquisitors held some spectacularly riotous parties here, and at such times would banish their domestic staff to nearby caves so that they could not bear witness to the drunkeness and lechery that would inevitably accompany such raves.

Zebbug is a small town that can trace its history back to the fifteenth century and possibly beyond. Like Lija, Attard and Balzan, many of its structures bear the showy yet graceful designs of medieval Maltese architecture, in particular the churches. The parish church is dedicated to St Philip; built in 1599, its exterior bears all the hallmarks of the plain, simply proportioned Mannerist style that was then so prevalent, but its interior has been given over to lavish Baroque. There are four other churches in Zebbug and although none are as physically impressive as St Philip's, each one has its own appeal. The arch to the north of the village, on the Valletta road, is dedicated to the penultimate Grandmaster of Malta, de Rohan. In the centre of Zebbug, near St Philip's, there are a few bars where one can stop for a drink and a snack.

A town very similar architecturally to Zebbug is **Siggiewi**, a short drive south of Zebbug itself. This primarily agricultural settlement is small and sleepy but does boast a parish church that was designed by no less than Lorenzo Gafa, creator of Mdina Cathedral. Unfortunately, much of Gafa's work has been disguised by later additions but it is still a lovely building, topped by an unusually high dome and dedicated to St Nicholas or, as he is otherwise known, Father Christmas. The church's interior is astounding, Baroque at its most extravagant. On St Margaret's Street one can see the house that belonged to the Secretary to the Inquisition; ask for the Villa Sant Cassia.

South of Siggiewi is the first opportunity this tour offers for a swim. Follow the signposted metal road to Ghar Lapsi, where there is a charming, secluded cove with two small rocky pools. There is also a small restaurant nearby. Further east of the cove, along the coastal road, are two fine prehistoric temple sites, situated closely together, Haqar Qim and Mnajdra. The Hagar Qim site has a car park and is just off the coastal road; Mnajdra is accessible only on foot from

Hagar Qim, a marvel of prehistoric engineering

Hagar Qim, a five-minute walk away along a stone track.

The **Mnajdra Temples** are the simpler of the two, yet this is somewhat compensated for by their quiet and atmospheric setting, on an open plateau gazing out to sea. There are three temples here, the first (on the right as one approaches) being a small trefoil affair that was constructed during the Ggantija Phase of around 3500BC and thus predating the Egyptian pyramids at Giza by approximately 1,000 years. The other two temples are larger and younger, built some 500 years later and in a design that broadly resembles that of the Ggantija temples on Gozo: a curved façade, an outer temple and an inner sanctuary. One is free to wander in and out of the temples, noting the sheer solidity of the structures and some of the decorative carvings that many of the stone blocks display. It is the left hand temple that is perhaps the most impressive, with its many altars and niches, its walls that climb up to 4m (13ft) in height and its artwork, many of the stones being engraved in distinctive, symmetrical patterns.

The Mnajdra Temples were constructed from tough coralline limestone, unlike **Hagar Qim** which is of the weaker globigerina. The advantage of globigerina to prehistoric man though, was that this is a type of limestone that is far easier to cut and to decorate and the designers of this complex exploited that benefit to the full. There are some tremendous examples of prehistoric art on display here. Yet this is not all that is impressive about Hagar Qim. The structure itself is a testimony to the ingenuity of the temple's engineers, huge megalithic blocks having been dragged into place to create a structure that has lasted some 5,500 years. The temple's design is essentially similar to other temples of the Ggantija Phase although numerous alterations and modifications by succeeding generations of worshippers has obscured much of what was original.

Looking out to sea from Hagar Qim one can see 3 miles (5km) offshore the tiny islet of **Filfla**, only a half-mile (1km) in circumference. Not surprisingly, it is uninhabited except for a variety of creatures that have taken advantage of the islet having recently been deemed a nature reserve. These include several species of sea-gulls and a lizard, *lacenta filfolemsis filfolemsis* or more easily, a type of gecko. In creating a nature reserve here, the Maltese are treating the islet with more respect than the British did during their tenure on Malta: they saw Filfla merely as a convenient place for their warships to get target practise and bombarded the islet practically to rubble.

Continuing east, a dirt road just about suitable for cars leads down past a row of touristic restaurants to a boat filled bay from where one can make the trip out to Malta's **Blue Grotto** (as distinct from Comino's Blue Grotto). Its very name attracts more visitors than this perhaps rather overrated sight deserves but nevertheless, if you like grottoes you will enjoy this one, with its aquamarine blue waves splashing gently against the smooth grey rocks.

From the grotto, turn north following the signs to **Zurrieq**, one of the oldest villages on Malta. As with most Maltese villages, the main focal point of interest here is its parish church, dedicated to St Catherine and built in the seventeenth century. Its exterior is unusual, a hotch-potch of styles and various modifications over the years but the wall paintings inside are a revelation, most of them the work of the brilliant Mattia Preti, creator of the stupendous interior of St John's Co-Cathedral in Valletta. Near the church is the Armeria, a grand house with an imposing watch tower that was designed as a palace but used by the Knights as an armoury. To the north of Zurrieq, the abandoned village of Hal Millieri has two churches one of which, the Church of the Assumption, has fine and recently renovated murals that were first painted in the fifteenth century.

Zurrieq marks the beginning of the end of the tour. Leave the village on the northern road marked Luqa, by-pass the village of Kirkop and one is within striking distance of Valletta. The road passes the international airport and at one point, dips underneath the main runway, an indication of how small an island Malta is. **Luqa** itself suffered horribly during World War II and although much has now been restored it still retains a quiet and desolate air. From here, there are two possible routes back through Hamrun and on to Valletta and Floriana. One such route passes through an industrial estate and as such, is not particularly pleasing aesthetically; the other is via Marsa Sports Club where a whole range of sports are on offer to both spectators and participants, from horse-racing to an 18-hole golf course.

Additional Information

Places to Visit

Attard
San Anton Palace and Gardens
Open: 8am-8pm daily.

Verdala Palace
Verdala Gardens
Open: 9am-12noon and 2-5pm
Tuesdays and Fridays.

Hagar Qim Temples and Mnajdra Temples
☎ 695578 (Directorate of Museums)
Open: winter, 8.15am-5.00pm
Monday-Saturday and 8.15am-4.15pm Sunday.
Summer, 7.45am-2.00pm daily.

5

THE EAST

Unlike parts of western Malta, great chunks of which have been sacrificed on tourism's altar, eastern Malta still belongs very much to the Maltese. This is not to say that it is boring or that there is nothing of interest here. The area boasts some of the finest and most fascinating sights on the island. The whole atmosphere is very different, much more relaxed and easy-going with the emphasis on getting on with local life, rather than catering for the whims of itinerants. So do not visit eastern Malta looking for carbon copies of Sliema and St Paul's; these types of places are just not to be found. Come instead to experience a region with a quite astonishing breadth of appeal. For in touring eastern Malta, the hardest-to-please traveller will find something to enjoy; and for the devoted sight-seer, it will be sheer delight.

The tour commences proper at the 'three cities' of Senglea, Vittoriosa and Cospicua, which occupy the seaward area east of Grand Harbour. The cities (more like small towns, really) are collectively known as the Cottonera, after Grandmaster Nicolas Cotonera fortified their landward approach with tremendous walls in the seventeenth century. There are some lovely spots here: Vittoriosa in particular, which the Knights of St John made their capital upon their arrival on Malta, holds a special kind of magic. It then moves on to Kalkara, almost at the north-eastern tip of Grand Harbour, before cutting around the coast and heading inland through the old village-cum-town of Zabbar to Marsascala on the western coast, which offers the chance of a swim. Return inland from here, via Zejtun with its fine old churches, to Tarxien and the substantial remains of temples that date back to prehistoric times. To sate the atmosphere for prehistoric Malta further, one can also visit in the Vallettan suburb of Paola and the Hypogeum, a series of underground burial

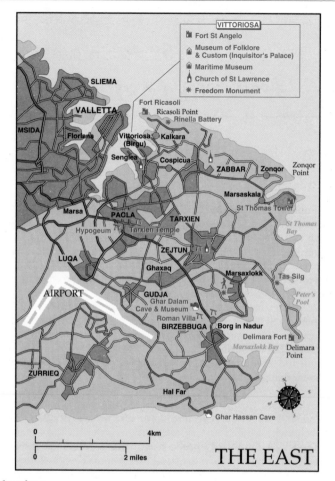

chambers.

Travel south-east from Tarxien towards the Cave of Ghar Dalam, and a geological incursion into a Malta that existed before man ever walked on the island. The cave is near Birzebbuga, where one can enjoy swimming and sunbathing on what is without doubt eastern Malta's finest sandy beach. From here, follow the coast around to another cave, the Ghar Hassan, before returning north again on the road back to the capital and the conclusion of the tour.

Much of this tour can be completed by public bus (check the bus map published by the Public Transport Authority for up-to-date details) although, of course, having one's own transport is by far the more preferable option. The exception to this rule are the 'three cities' which, due to the spaghetti-like nature of their streets and their parking problems, are far better explored on foot.

The Tour

From Valletta, there are two ways to reach the 'three cities'. The first is by the romantic option, quietly crossing the calm blue waters of Grand Harbour to Vittoriosa in the same way that Dun Salv, Monserrat's *kappillan* in *The Kappillan of Malta* travelled, on those small, colourful Maltese ferries, the *dghajjes*. Unfortunately, however, a *dghajsa* can be hard to find these days (although you may strike lucky, especially if you are in a large group and can charter one) and so most travellers are forced to fall back on the second, rather more mundane option, which is to take a bus from Valletta's main city gate.

On the eastern side of Grand Harbour, two long fingers of land protrude outwards towards Valletta: Senglea occupies the southerly finger, Vittoriosa the northerly and between and on either side of them are sheltered three, natural deep water harbours, French Creek, Dockyard Creek and Kalkara Creek. The final city of the trio, Cospicua, is located on the landward side behind the two, providing defence from the rear. There is a beautiful, yet somewhat faded charm to all 'three cities' that mingles with a certain sense of melancholy. For this area, due to its creeks providing for ships the safest anchorage on the island, bore the brunt of the German bombing duing World War II and even now, fifty years on, the damage is still all too evident. Yet the 'three cities' survived all that the *Luftwaffe* could hurl at them and today they thrive, as they have done for over half a millennium.

Upon arriving on Malta, the Knights found only two cities in which to settle. One was Mdina, unsuitable as a capital as it was positioned too far from the sea for the Order's fleet and was the preserve of the Maltese nobility anyway. The second was Vittoriosa, then called Birgu, a rather down-at-heel settlement with delapidated defences but which at least had the advantage of bisecting two deep creeks that were ideal for the Knights' galleys. The Knights' settled on the latter and, knowing that a Turkish attack in the near future was inevitable, set about re-constructing the city, fortifying it and building *auberges* and edifices suitably sumptious for what was after all, the most esteemed and noble of all the European Orders. At around the same time construction began on Senglea, named after Grandmaster de la Sengle: Cospicua, then the village of Bormla, was for the time being left as it was, a small and muddy hamlet.

As their capital city, Birgu was the Knights base during the Great Siege of 1565 and in the euphoria that came with the victory, the city was renamed Vittoriosa, 'the victorious'. Senglea too, got a new name, Invitta or 'the unconquered', although no one ever refers to it as such today. Indeed, even the name Vittoriosa has had a hard time catching on. To the Maltese it is still Birgu and on maps of the area even today, the two names appear side by side.

The Turks were never again to attack Malta in force but the Knights fear of a repeat of the Great Siege never dissipated. As late as the eighteenth century, Grandmaster Nicolas Cottonera ordered that the Cottonera Lines be built, a vast half moon-shaped wall that enclosed Bormla and the landward entrances to Senglea and Vittoriosa. Accordingly Bormla boomed and the town received the name, Cospicua, or 'the conspicuous'. Today it is rather less than its honorific suggests, little more than a residential suburb for those who work in Valletta or in the ship repair yards around the 'three cities'. For the deep water creeks of the 'three cities' are far too precious a national asset for the Maltese to waste and the area is still, as it was in the days of the Knights, the centre of the nation's heavy shipping industry.

✳ Queen of the 'three cities' is **Vittoriosa-Birgu** and any visitor with time for only one of the trio should make this the one. Apart from the fine sights outlined below, there are a wealth of smaller curiosities, a Norman house here, a fine church there, all awaiting discovery by those prepared to merely wander through its quiet and slender streets. The suburb, like all great Maltese cities, has a main gate that dates back to medieval times but for the purposes of this tour, one does not enter Vittoriosa through it. Instead, the tour begins at the end of St Tereza's Street on the southern approach to the city, where the road hugs Dockyard Creek, looking across its waters to the sister promontory of Senglea.

As the creek's name suggests, this is dockyard land. Marsa, with its great ship repair yards, may be the home of the Maltese shipping today but this is the area where it was originally born. Indeed, it is fitting that it is at this point where the Maltese government chose to ✳ erect the Freedom Monument, which commemorates the withdrawl of the British from the island in 1979. Standing amidst a garden of flowers in front of a richly Baroque church, the monument bears four figures: a Maltese hoisting the flag, a bugler sounding the farewell and a British sailor saying goodbye to a Maltese docker. Below the monument is dry dock number one, the first and the smallest of the dry docks built here. Across the water in Senglea the huge, crumbling dockside buildings have been used for a variety of sea-faring purposes, whether as an arsenal for the Knights galleys or as hostels for the British engineers. Along the street there are a handful of dark, down-at-heel but welcoming bars, that would have been well patronised by sailors not so very long ago. Everywhere there are traces of faded glory, remnants of the days when Malta was the undisputed naval centre of the Mediterranean.

The Baroque church that the Freedom Monument stands before is the loveliest in Vittoriosa. This is the Church of St Lawrence, originally built by the Normans in the eleventh century and enriched by the Knights in 1530, when it became the conventual church of the Order. Virtually nothing remains of the edifice from this era however, because in 1691 Lorenzo Gafa, mastermind of the cathedrals at Mdina and at Victoria on Gozo, completely rebuilt the church in lavish Baroque. The style and grace of Gafa's design is all too evident in its exterior, but as is usual with the great Baroque churches of Malta, it is the softly lit interior that steals the show, embellished as it is with red marble and covered with intricate, gentle paintings. The small chapel nearby is dedicated to St Joseph, in which is displayed the hat and sword of arguably the greatest of the Grandmasters, Jean de La Valette. Unfortunately, this chapel may well be locked — the church is only used once a year, on 8 September, the anniversary of Turkish retreat.

The Chapel of St Joseph borders the Piazza Vittoriosa (Vittoriosa Square) the centre of the suburb and the focal point for the festivities during the 10 August *festa* of St Lawrence, when the square is festooned with colourful banners and papier mache statues of the saints. At other times, it seems almost bleak with only a handful of monuments to catch the eye. Most impressive is the white stone statue of St Lawrence himself, although the Victory Monument, topped by a statue of a Knight in armour, is not far behind. It commemorates the victory of the Great Siege and was erected by the Knights in 1705, 140 years after the event itself. Also in the square is a stone crucifix, marking the spot where prisoners condemned to death were publicly executed in those hard, harsh days.

Leaving the square, return to the Freedom Monument, pass under the small medieval gate nearby to the east and walk down the wharf alongside Dockyard Creek. The first attraction here is not long in presenting itself, located within a grand old building that once served as the Bakery, where bread and biscuits for the British sailors based here were baked. Now it houses the Maritime Museum of Malta, a carefully planned museum that traces the maritime history of Malta with considerable style. Among its vast array of artefacts are delicate, precise models of ships, from the *luzzi* to Knights galleys to British destroyers, the uniforms worn by a Captain and an Admiral of the Knights of St John, medieval navigational devices, some truly immense anchors and a selection of cannons, including two left over from the French occupation of Malta that bear the inscription, 'Republic of France'.

Of the buildings along Dockyard Creek, it was not just the Bakery that was once under the control of the British. Many of them served, in one function or another, as Royal Naval administrative offices. This was their function under the Knights of St John too and one can still see the original Treasury of the Order, the Captain General's Palace, the Arsenal Administration building and the Hostel for Captains of the Galleys. Sadly, most of these fine buildings now stand in virtual ruin, shattered by German bombing during World War II. On some buildings one can see only the ugly pittings and pockmarks of shrapnel; on others, great chunks of masonry have been smashed away. Indeed, the only relics of the past along Dockyard Creek that seem to have escaped damage are the bollards which are worth a close look as they are, in fact, the barrels of muzzle-loaded cannons.

Nearing the end of a wharf, go up a small ramp and over a bridge that crosses the only surviving moat on Malta, a moat that forms part

Dramatic and imposing, the Church of St Lawrence in Vittoriosa

of the defences of one of the most important forts on the island, Fort
St Angelo. Sadly, the Fort is now closed to visitors (although this may
change in the future) but its fine battlements are superbly impressive, displaying upon them a bell that was brought by the Knights
from Rhodes and which was rung continuously for a whole day
upon the lifting of the Great Siege. No one can be exactly sure for how
long a fortress has stood on this site, some estimates claim for at least
2,000 years, but it seems certain that the Saracens had fortifications
here. The Normans developed these further and the Knights, never
ones to leave defences to chance, completed the process and constructed a castle that, following the fall of St Elmo during the Great
Siege, withstood the most ferocious of Turkish attacks. During the
period of British rule on Malta, it served as an administration centre
for the Royal Navy and from 1933 onwards was the Headquarters for
the Commander of the Fleet, Mediterranean arena, acquiring that

*The narrow streets of
Vittoriosa draped with
banners for the* festa

same year that most renowned of naval honours, ship status, with the launch of the Royal Navy's *HMS St Angelo*. Despite being directly hit nearly seventy times during the German bombing offensive of 1942 the fort suffered relatively little damage and indeed, when one gazes up at the solid battlements, bristling with bastions, the impression is of a bulwark that could last forever. Inside is the Chapel of St Anne within whose crypt were originally buried four of the early Grandmasters. At this point, retrace one's steps back along the wharf to the Freedom Monument and from there, to Piazza Vittoriosa. Those who wish to see Fort St Angelo from a different angle need only to walk due west from here, towards the end of the promontory, and to cross a small bridge over the moat to its plain but sturdy gate.

As the old city centre, it was only natural that the eight *langues* of the Knights should build their *auberges* near Piazza Vittoriosa. The *auberge* of Allemagne was actually built on the square itself but sadly, was destroyed by German bombing in 1942. Other *auberges* however, despite most being damaged in the raids, were more fortunate and still stand today, albeit in variable states of repair. In an architectural sense, they can in no way compare with the great *auberges* of Valletta and give the impression of being built in a hurry, without any careful attention to style. To view them, leave Piazza Vittoriosa at its northern end, on Hilda Tabone Street.

The first *auberge* on this street belonged to the English, a *langue* that failed to survive the Reformist reign of King Henry VIII. Its design shows echoes of the Mannerist style, such as in the circular window above its entrance, but overall it is not particularly impressive. The same can be said of the *auberge* opposite it, which once housed the Knights of Auvergne and Provence, *langues* who, seeing as they shared the same language, felt that they may as well share the same building. Better is the *auberge* of France, further along the street and with some pleasing decoration, most notably around the doorway. Behind this *auberge*, the Benedictine Convent was once the original *Sacre Infermeria*, the first hospital the Knights of St John built on Malta and one handed over to the Benedictines after the completion of the hospital in Valletta. Lovers of the artist Mattia Preti may want to visit the convents church, St Scholastica, where the altarpiece is the work of the great man.

From the square, walk east up Main Gate Street where, two blocks along, there is a large building whose dark and foreboding appearance seems to tell a thousand stories of the horrors that were perpetrated within its walls. During the time of the Knights this was the most feared and hated building on the island, a place from where few who entered ever left: for this was the Palace of the Papal Inquisitor.

The palace was not built especially for the men of the Inquisition. Originally it was a normal courthouse, the Castellania, and it was only in 1574 that the Inquisitors arrived on the island to take up residence there. They had come to ensure that the Knights were still loyally Catholic during a time in which Luther's Reformist ideals were sweeping Europe and, although they found the Knights as orthodox as ever, proved impossible to shift. Between 1574 and 1798, sixty-two Inquisitors were appointed by the Papacy to serve on Malta, and each one was as hated by the islanders as the last. Men and women were imprisoned, tortured and executed without even knowing what the charges against them were and tales abound of Knights ransacking the palace and freeing imprisoned friends from dungeons in which they were held in the most horrific conditions imaginable. At no time however, was an Inquisitor actually harmed: he was an appointee of the Pope and despite their wary mistrust of Rome, the Knights were nothing if not firmly Catholic.

The palace suffered badly from the German bombing, as can be seen in its shrapnel-pitted walls, but has since been restored as a Folklore and Custom Museum. The dungeons are still there, some of the cells bearing the scratched graffiti marks of prisoners, as is the court house with its entrance built deliberately low, so that the accused would be forced to enter bowing to the Grand Inquisitor. Many of the other rooms however, are very grand; graceful windows, beamed ceilings and gentle Baroque decoration. In common with many of their masters in the Vatican, the Inquisitors enjoyed a life of opulence.

From its inception, the Inquisition was dominated by the Dominican Order. It was convenient for the Grand Inquisitor therefore, that the Cominican Church of the Annunciation stood and still stands only a few steps away from the portaled palace door. The original church had to be virtually entirely re-built after the bombing of World War II but its replacement echoes what went before, having been designed in heavy, almost overbearing Baroque. Its altarpiece is the work of no less than Mattia Preti. Next door is the Dominican Priory.

The main gate of Vittoriosa, or gates, as there are actually three of them, are only a short walk east from here, at the end of Main Gate Street. These gates were built with defence as the prime consideration. All three lie along Covered Gate Street, which twists its narrow way in and out of the city, crossing a small bridge en route. The gates themselves are well worth pausing to examine, being fine examples of eighteenth-century workmanship. Leaving the city, the first one passed under is Vittoriosa Gate, modestly built and without any real distinguishing architectural features. Next comes the elegant Couvre Porte, the 'covered gate' itself and finally, Advanced Gate which has the date of its construction, 1722, inscribed in Roman numerals above it.

✳ **Senglea,** on the other side of Dockyard Creek, was pulverised during World War II. As with Vittoriosa, this was an area totally devoted to shipping, and as such received special attention from the *Luftwaffe*. Much of the suburb had to be totally re-built following the war although no amount of bombing could totally destroy the vista that lies at the easternmost tip of Senglea, which is arguably one of the most spectacular that Malta has to offer. Orientating oneself is easy here: Senglea's street lay-out follows the symmetrical, grid-plan Vallettan pattern, with a single main street, Victory Street, running through its centre from its fine, medieval gate to the promontory's

All but impenetrable, the mighty Advanced Gate of Vittoriosa

end; note that unless one feels some overwhelming urge to explore, there is no real need to leave this thoroughfare.

It takes no genius to guess what victory the Church of the Victory, a short stroll down the main street from Senglea's gate, commemorates. This was first built in the immediate aftermath of the Great Siege and stood for nearly 400 years, before being smashed by German bombs. Today it has been re-built, in heavy Baroque and although it is by no means the finest church on Malta, a peek inside is well rewarded by the painstaking work that has gone into its altar, embellished as it is with wood and marble carvings and covered by a four-posted canopy. For a church that survived the last war, take a look at the seventeenth-century Church of St Philip, at the western end of Victory Street.

Behind St Philip's at the very tip of the promontory are the Safe Haven Gardens, although it is disputable whether 'gardens' is the right word to describe this patch of concrete, jazzed up by a few plants here and there. Visit them though, because the view of Grand Harbour from here is astounding. Ahead, across the calm waters, are the mighty sea walls of Valletta and Floriana and immediately to the right in Vittoriosa is Fort St Angelo. Beyond the fort is the entrance to Grand Harbour, much of it sealed off by a breakwater, while far to the left are the great shipyards of Marsa. Below, boats small and large

The fortified gate of Senglea

criss-cross the harbour. It is a quite stunning vista and one perhaps best enjoyed from the *vedette* that hangs over the edge of the garden's walls, an hexagonal sentry post built by the Knights of St John and with decorations in stone relief depicting what a sentry should use most — eyes and ears.

There is not a great deal to see in **Cospicua**, aside from what remains of the Cotonera Lines, the brainchild of Grandmaster Nicolas Cotonera. Cotonera was a Grandmaster who hated the Turks even more than most — his monumental tomb in St John's Co-Cathedral in Valletta is supported by statues of two cowering Turkish slaves — and it was his fear of another Ottoman assault on the Order that led him to direct (and pay for) the construction of this great land wall. Curving around in a protective embrace of the 'three cities', its total length is nearly 3 miles (5km) but it was never quite finished; Cotonera died before its completion and his successor felt that quite enough money had been spent on the lines already. Most of its gates are now sealed up although one, the carefully carved Zabbar gate is open to traffic heading for that small town. The gate's inscription notes that these great walls were the gift of Grandmaster Cotonera.

Kalkara, a small fishing village north of the 'three cities', has an impossibly pretty little harbour which still in part serves its traditional role as the shelter of the traditional Maltese ferry boats, the *dghajjes*. Cushioned between Kalkara Creek and Rinella Creek, the village's delightful appearance and easy access to commercial Malta have turned it into a popular place to live and its surrounds are filled with half-completed houses being built by those who have bought plot of land here. Devoted sight-seers, however, will find little to keep them in Kalkara and will want to travel still further north, out of the village and following the signs to the **Rinella Battery**, at a site that guards the entrance to Grand Harbour. The Battery is an immense, muzzle-loading gun, weighing in at 100 tons and was positioned there by the British at a time when the Italian fleet was growing in power to an extent that the British thought they may attempt a quick raid on Malta, with the intention of stealing the island for themselves. The raid never materialised but still the gun stands there, its barrel gazing out to sea.

West of the Rinella Battery, at the fingernail of a promontory that curves around almost far enough to turn Grand Harbour into an inland sea, is **Fort Ricasoli**. Paid for by the Knight Francesco Ricasoli, it was designed in the seventeenth century by the same engineer that built the Cotonera Lines. Today the fort is closed but nevertheless, the views from its surrounds are particularly lovely. Many scenes from the film *Raise the Titanic*, adapted from the book by Clive

Cussler, were shot here. From the fort, return to Kalkara and take the road via Il-Wileg to the small town of **Zabbar**.

After landing at Marsaxlokk in 1565, the Turks made their first camp at Zabbar, which today is a quiet and peaceful suburb surrounded by farmlands. With its slender streets and alleys, Zabbar is a pleasant place to wander around, new houses easily intermingling with those built centuries before and has a quite splendid seventeenth-century church dedicated to Our Lady of Grace. This is a large, imposing, almost fortress-like structure with a great barrel-vaulted ceiling with a small museum attached, displaying various samples of religious bric-a-brac. At the eastern side of the town, the Hompesch Arch stands rather improbably alone in the middle of a traffic island. This arch is virtually all that physically remains from the tenure of Grandmaster de Hompesch.

Marsascala, on the coast east of Zabbar, is a modern little town with pretensions to becoming a tourist resort. Those who visit though, may well be disappointed by the swimming opportunities on offer here — just a few flat rocks either side of the harbour to bathe off. Better swimming is to be had at St Thomas Bay, a ten-minute walk to the south. Marsascala's history can be seen in the Zonqor Tower to the north of the harbour, and in St Thomas Tower to the south, both constructed during the seventeenth century. St Thomas, near the Jerma Palace Hotel, has since been converted into a good restaurant.

Zejtun, a large inland village south-west of Marsascala, draws its name from the Arabic for 'olive' as in past times, this whole area was plastered with olive trees. Olive oil production, however, was not the ideal produce for Malta. The island is just too small to accommodate hectare after hectare of olive trees in an area such as the Mediterranean, whose nations have always produced olive oil in vast quantities, consequently keeping its price low. Zejtun is an antiquitous village — the remains of a Roman villa have been discovered beneath a local school — but sight-wise it is best known for its two fine churches, both near each other in the village centre. The seventeenth-century parish church is dedicated to St Catherine and is a domed, heavily Baroque affair that towers majestically over everything in its immediate vicinity. A short walk away, the Church of St Gregory is one of the oldest surviving churches on Malta, first built in 1436. The Knights of St John did their best to add a few frills to the edifice but they could not quite overcome the stark, straightforward style in which it was constructed.

Tarxien, west of Zejtun, also has a church but few visitors to the town go there to see it. They visit instead for the temples, which

A moment for quiet reflection at Kalkara Creek

The prehistoric temples of Tarxien

The sacrificial altar at the prehistoric temple complex, Tarxien

The Church of Our Lady of Grace in Zabbar, typical of the Baroque style of architecture

represent what is considered by many to be the height of prehistoric civilisation on Malta. Built around 2400BC, the temples lay buried beneath the soil for some 3,500 years, until a farmer discovered them by accident in 1915. There are three temples here, thanks to renovation all in a comparatively good state of repair and one does not need to stretch the imagination far to imagine them as they were. Even those pieces that have been moved to the National Archaeology Museum in Valletta have been replaced with replicas, thus preserving further the authenticity of the site.

The first temple, designed to the standard four apse plan, is entered through a free standing arch. This is where the bulk of the best-known finds at Tarxien were unearthed, such as the 'fat lady', of which only the lower part remains. In its complete form this fertility statue would have stood over 2m (7ft) high: what one sees here though, is a copy; the original is in Valletta. Likewise the altar niche, at the northern end of the temple, with its small window-type cavity cut into its side. A small, flint sacrificial knife was discovered inside this cavity during the excavations at Tarxien and behind the altar itself, were charred and splintered bones of sacrificed animals. This first temple also contains some of the best examples yet discovered of prehistoric art, great stone blocks adorned with carefully carved animals and primitive ships, as well as the distinctive horned spirals.

The second temple is the larger of the group. Carefully planned, with a floor of stone slabs, it is divided into three distinct apses and centred with a large circular hearth, cracked by fire. It may have been offerings that were burnt here, or possibly aromatic herbs in order to create a prehistoric incense. There are more stone carvings in relief here, all of which strongly point to the temple having fertility worship as its focus — a bull, and a sow suckling her litter. It takes some effort to clamber up over the stones into a separate complex at the north-eastern side of this temple, into an area which may have been the sole preserve of the priests. There is little to see in the third temple, just the remains of its walls although beyond it are the scanty remains of yet another temple, possibly the first one built on this site and dating from the Ggantija phase.

There are two reasons why one may want to visit the rather less than enticing suburb of **Paola**, just west of Tarxien. The first is if you happen to fall foul of Maltese law — the island's prison is here. The second is to view the Hypogeum of Hal Saflieni, an underground complex of prehistoric burial chambers, the precursor, if you like, of St Paul's Catacombs underneath Rabat. Like the Tarxien temples, these too were discovered by accident, by workmen digging foundations for a house in 1902. The workmen initially kept their find to themselves — to have broadcast the news would have undoubtedly led to the British administration ordering a halt to the building, thus putting them out of a job — but it could not remain secret for long and within a few years, the chambers existence had become common knowledge. Work on the excavations began in earnest.

The Hypogeum (which means 'under the earth') was hollowed out of the soft globegerina limestone by prehistoric man around 2400BC, using simple tools of bone and flint and it is estimated that over the years, some 7,000 corpses were interred here. Initially, the burial chambers were built near the surface but as time progressed, and space for more bodies began to run short, its builders dug deeper until this labyrinthical network extended down through three separate storeys. The earliest, uppermost level is the least impressive, the chambers being roughly hewn and confused by the foundation walls of neighbouring houses intruding into the site. The careless, pick-axe wielding workmen who built these houses also did a fair amount of damage, particularly around the entrance.

However, they thankfully left the rest of the Hypogeum untouched and it is here, at the middle and lower levels, that the hushed, almost ethereal atmosphere of the site comes to the fore. Nowhere is this better illustrated than at the middle level, which was used in part as a temple and which bears abundant signs of prehistoric decoration in the red ochre painted ceiling and in the irregular squares and stripes, spirals and dots scratched onto its walls. Chief of the sites here is the 'Holy of Holies', a chamber carved out of the rock in the curved shape of a temple's apse. It is from the 'Holy of Holies' that one descends further into the bowels of the Hypogeum to the lower storey, a labyrinth of carefully cut burial chambers. Leaving the Malta of yesteryear behind, leave Paola on the Birzebbuga road and bear left, after the turn off to Zejtun, to the coastal town of Marsaxlokk.

Marsaxlokk has been a popular place amongst the invaders of ✳ Malta; the Turks landed here in 1565, so too did Napoleon in 1798. Today, however, its invaders come armed only with swimsuits and sun-tan oil to enjoy this one-time small fishing village that is fast adapting to its new role of holiday resort. It is certainly a picturesque enough place, despite its lack of a beach, with an impossibly quaint harbour filled with *luzzi* and a plethora of fine fish restaurants, Skuna, Harbour Lights and Hunter's Tower to name but three. Those who prefer to cook their own fish can choose their supper at the fish market, held at the harbourside every Sunday morning. There is a market on other mornings too, but they are less smelly and concentrate on selling souvenirs such as lace-work and knit-wear. Marsaxlokk has something of a reputation as a heat-trap: indeed, its name is derived from *marsa* meaning 'harbour' and *xlokk* meaning 'scirroco' making it in English 'the harbour of the hot wind'.

Sights-wise, there is not a great deal to see, although one can enjoy a lovely walk from the village to **Delimara Point** at the easternmost tip of Malta. The point was fortitfied in only the seventeenth century, by the still-standing Fort Delimara Tower. The walk passes the fast growing holiday resort of Tas Silg, where prehistoric and Roman remains have been unearthed, and Peter's Pool where one can bathe from smooth, flat rocks in waters deep and beautifully clear. An equally pleasant walk is to be had south of Marsaxlokk, rounding the coastline on the way to Birzebbuga. En route is the St Lucian Tower (now a fish-farming laboratory), twin sentinel of Delimara Fort, and also built in the seventeenth century to guard both sides of Marsaxlokk's sheltered harbour. This coastal road south of Marsaxlokk comes out at the junction of the Valletta-Birzebbuga road. Turn right here and a short distance up on the left is the entrance to **Ghar Dalam**, the 'Cave of Darkness', a visit to which takes one back to the very dawn of time.

One enters the site at the museum before descending a long series of steps down the side of a valley to the cave itself. Prehistoric Malta

Horned spirals decorate the stones of Tarxien

was a lot rainier than it is today and the waters cut a river into a part of the valley where the rock was at its softest. Over the years, the rain washed the bones of those prehistoric animals who had died in the valley into the river and when the waters eventually dried up, all that was left was a long cave filled with the remains of these creatures. The cave, dark and cool, is open to visitors and one can follow the course of the prehistoric river through 80m (262ft) of its length.

Above the valley, the Ghar Dalam Museum exhibits the animal bones that were found in the cave. The principle 'more is beautiful' clearly has been applied here for where one hippo, red deer or mammoth bone would do, there are literally thousands on display, stacked up one on top of the other inside large glass cabinets. More interesting are the skeletons that are on display, even though these are copies, not originals — a brown bear, an elephant, a wolf and a hippopotamus, among others. The elephants and hippos are of the 'pygmy' variety, probably due to the poor supply of food on the island which would have stunted their growth.

Ask at the museum for directions to the nearby prehistoric site of Borg In-Nadur, where there is a long megalithic wall that was built around 1400BC. The remains of a temple and a few huts have also been found here and there are some cart ruts, too. The wall was presumably built for defensive purposes although who these settlers were defending against, is unknown.

Birzebbuga is now the biggest holiday resort on the eastern coast, although it still has a long way to go to rival the likes of St Paul's and Sliema. It is not hard to ascertain the source of this town's popularity; the beach here is the best in the area, big and sandy but somewhat spoiled by the view from it, which is of the island's largest freeport container harbour. Offshore are two oil rigs from which the Maltese, with fingers firmly crossed, are drilling for oil. It was on a warship off the coast of Birzebbuga that now ex-Presidents Bush and Gorbachev met for a summit in 1988 and at the harbourside, a monument commemorates the event.

This tour of eastern Malta could end here, although cave freaks may enjoy a trip south to a cave named after its one-time occupant **Ghar Hassan**. Who Hassan was is open to question — most say he was an eleventh-century Saracen — but whoever he was, he was clearly a man not fussy about the standard of his accommodation. The cave is clammy and cold and muddy, with little to see inside except for rock walls oozing water. He was also a man with an unsavoury side to his character. Lacking an honest profession, Hassan made a living out of capturing young girls and selling them to the captains of passing ships as slaves. By means of advertising, he would suspend the girls on ropes over the side of the cliff at the mouth of the cave so that the sailors could examine their purchases more closely: and if, after a while, a girl remained unsold, then snip! The rope would be cut and down she would plunge. Or so they say. A torch is needed to explore the cave properly. If you have not got one, there are several for hire in a hut by the road at the approach to the cave.

Additional Information

Places to Visit

Birzebbuga

Ghar Dalam *Cave and Museum*
Zejtun Road
☎ 824419
Open: winter 8.15am-5pm Monday to Saturday and 8.15am-4.15pm Sunday. Summer 7.45am-2pm daily.

Ghar Hassan

Near Hal Far
Open: winter 8.15am-5pm Monday to Saturday and 8.15am-4.15pm Sunday. Summer 7.45am-2pm daily.

Paola

Hal-Saflieni Hypogeum
Burials Street
☎ 825579
Open: winter 8.15am-5pm Monday to Saturday and 8.15am-4.15pm Sunday. Summer 7.45am-2pm daily.

Tarxien

Temples
Old Temples Street
☎ 695578
Open: winter 8.15am-5pm Monday to Saturday and 8.15am-4.15pm Sunday. Summer 7.45am-2pm daily.

Vittoriosa

Maritime Museum
The Naval Bakery
☎ 805287
Open: winter, 8.15am-5pm Monday to Saturday. 8.15am-4.15pm Sunday. Summer, 7.45am-2pm daily.

Museum of Folklore and Custom
Palace of the Papal Inquisitor
Main Gate Street
☎ 827006
Open: winter 8.15am-5pm Monday to Saturday and 8.15am-4.15pm Sunday. Summer 7.45am-2pm daily.

6

GOZO AND COMINO

Gozo ('Ghawdex' in Malti, pronounced 'Owdesh') is a gentle island. Separated from Malta by an 8km (5 mile) wide channel, it is less than half the size of its big brother yet seems far more spacious and free. There are fewer roads, cars, people and buildings; it is hard to feel crowded on quiet and peaceful Gozo. Some may find the island a little too quiet and peaceful; it has a few tourist 'sights' but not many, and although there are a handful of established resorts, the island's night life is definitely low-key. The day life is too, and during afternoon siesta, visitors could be forgiven for wondering whether the island was actually populated at all. Yet most of its visitors do not come to Gozo to party. They come to enjoy what the island offers best; a charming landscape, wonderful for walks outside the hot months of July and August; some fine spots for swimming and scuba diving; a fascinating old capital, the Citadel of Victoria; the happy hospitality of the Gozitans; and the chance to simply relax, and to soak up the atmosphere of an island that is similar, yet still undeniably different, to Malta.

Gozo is green, a rural island with, some claim, rural values. It has none of the cosmopolitan buzz of Valletta, Sliema and St Pauls. Its residents are renowned for their earthy qualities, their self-sufficiency and their honesty; indeed, for years, no one in Gozo bothered locking their doors. Perhaps it is a reflection of this that the most popular souvenirs on sale are those that are crafted in homes — hand-knitted sweaters, lace-work and Gozitan wine, the latter of which takes some getting used to but packs a powerful punch. The island earns its living from agriculture, nature having bestowed it with rich underlying deposits of blue clay, leaving the soil far more fertile than that on Malta. Its landscape too, lends itself to farming. Whereas Malta is a low and bumpy island, Gozo has genuine hills,

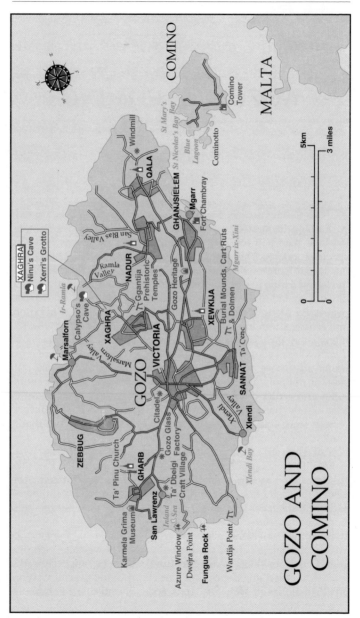

GOZO AND COMINO

many of them with flat, table-top peaks, meaning that its fields are sheltered from the fierce north-westerly winds that have so devastated the landscape on the northern coast of the island.

Yet despite being rich agriculturally, Gozo's reputation is as the poor relation of Malta. The chief buyer of its farm produce has always been the main island (although potatoes are now being exported to the Netherlands) and there is little in the way of industry. For what Gozo possesses in good farmland, it lacks in good harbours and its coastline has none of the deep, sheltered bays and creeks that Malta is so blessed with. It has therefore, been unable to share in all that has made Malta prosperous — ship repairing, for example, and foreign trade. Its population of 26,000 is enough to run the farms and sail the fishing boats but leaves little room for expansion in other directions. This is unlikely to change as, with many young Gozitans leaving for the faster life on Malta, its population seems set to decrease further.

Historically, Gozo has shared the same occupiers and inhabitants as Malta. With the discovery of the huge temples at Ggantija, it too can claim a prehistoric heritage certainly as old as Malta's and possibly older. Islanders claim that the fair and sexually licentious

Approaching the harbour at Mgarr

goddess Calypso, from Homer's epic *The Odyssey*, had her cave here, where she entrapped Odysseus, Homer's hero, for seven long years. Lacking the harbours and bays of Malta though, meant that Gozo was usually neglected when fortifications had to be built and Turkish pirates, if thwarted by the strong defences of Malta, would only have to sail through the channel to Gozo to find easy pickings. In 1546 the Gozitans, who were tiring of being constantly pillaged, burned the corpse of a captured Turkish corsair atop their Citadel, as a warning to other pirates watching that they had had enough. This turned out to be a bad move.

The Turk they had burnt was the brother of Dragut Reis, the cruellest and most feared of all the corsairs. Within five years he had a terrible revenge. Dragut landed on Gozo, subdued the island swiftly and carried what he thought was the entire population off to slavery. A few managed to evade capture though and they, together with those who eventually made their way home, kept the island going. Later, the Knights of St John put up a few desultory defences but the Turkish raids were to continue for years, right up to the eighteenth century. Gozo's suffering at the hands of the Turks was partly compensated for nearly 400 years later when the German bombers, who had little reason to attack Gozo when a huge shipyard and harbour awaited their bombs at Valletta, mostly ignored the island.

Car ferries leave for Gozo from Cirkewwa, at the north-western tip of Malta, regularly throughout the day with the crossing taking roughly thirty minutes. Less frequently, a ferry departs from Valletta, with the journey time taking around ninety minutes. All boats to Gozo arrive at Mgarr. The only other means of getting there is by helicopter from Luqa airport, perhaps not quite as expensive as one may suspect and certainly the most exciting way to arrive on Gozo. Regarding accommodation on the island, there are plenty of places to stay. Marsalforn, the chief resort, has the most accommodation possibilities for the independent traveller but the capital, Victoria, has hotels and nearly all the other towns and large villages have at least a guest house. Sannat, to the south of the island, has a de luxe five-star hotel, the Ta' Cenc. A full list of what is available can be obtained from tourist offices. Gozo's restaurants tend to be very good, particularly those specialising in traditional Maltese fare, and several are referred to in this chapter.

Gozo is small — 9 miles (15km) long and 4 miles (7km) wide — but getting around the island can be problematic. Buses run regularly between Mgarr and Victoria, departures coinciding with the ferry schedule, but otherwise the service is in no way as extensive as that on Malta. In theory, buses should be able to take you from Victoria to any village on the island; in practise, this is not quite the case. Many buses run only three of four times a day, and then to no real timetable. Consequently, it is better to hire a car or motorbike and see Gozo under your own steam; roads are well marked and, being so small, it is almost impossible to get lost. Alternatively, you could walk; the furthest distance on the island is no more than a three-hour stroll.

To fully appreciate the unique, sleepy, charmful atmosphere of Gozo, one needs a few days. To just see the sights though, and to get a small taste of the island, one day is sufficient and this is the amount of time most visitors allot to Gozo. Therefore, the tour outlined below begins and ends in the way most daytrips to Gozo do; at Mgarr harbour.

The Tour

Mgarr is no place to linger. A small and not particularly attractive village, its interest to visitors lies only in its man-made harbour and in the Sea View restaurant, which enjoys an excellent reputation for serving fine, fresh fish. Otherwise, press on. Before leaving though, gaze up to the hill overlooking the harbour where two structures compete for that hill's most prominent building. One is the neo-Gothic church of Our Lady of Lourdes — look for the statue of the Virgin Mary placed in a niche in the cliff below the church; the other is **Fort Chambray**. Built in the mid-eighteenth century, this fort was built by Jaques de Chambray, a one-time Admiral of the Knights who was later appointed Governor of Gozo. It represents one of the few serious attempts to fortify this island and was to see action when the French troops of Napoleon landed in 1798; for Chambray was the only fort on either Malta or Gozo to offer resistance.

Two roads lead out of Mgarr. One bears to the right, up to the small village of Qala; the other goes left and then straight, leading to the capital, Victoria. Taking this latter road, the suburbs of Mgarr soon become those of the village of **Ghanjsielem**, where the Gozo Heritage offers a good introduction to Gozo. A sight and sound show with a difference, a visit here enables newcomers to place all the sites of the island in their proper historical perspective. Visitors walk through the museum, where cleverly illuminated life-size model figures and a booming commentary takes them through the 6,000 years of the islands history.

From Ghanjsielm, Victoria is only a short drive away, beyond the large village of Xewkija. For the purposes of this tour though, return to the junction with Mgarr and climb upwards to **Qala**, a small agricultural village dominated by a large windmill, still with its sails and in working condition. Its church, the Sanctuary of the Immaculate Conception, has an exterior defaced or enhanced, depending upon your opinion, by graffiti from medieval times depicting ships from that era. Just before the village, there is a fine viewing spot, overlooking not only Mgarr harbour but also the Blue Lagoon of Comino, with its brilliant colour. From Qala a dirt road leads down through a gorge to a very small but secluded pebble beach, Pomegranate Beach. The road is difficult to find and you may have to enlist the help of locals. The pomegranates, alas, grow there no longer.

West of Qala, travelling inland, is **Nadur**, one of the largest villages on Gozo and with an attractive neo-Baroque parish church. The village's name is derived from the Arabic *nadar* or 'look-out' and

The well-preserved windmill at Qala

indeed, from its heights one can see vast chunks of the island and be able to appreciate the stark differences that exist between the Maltese and Gozitan landscapes. The omnipresent dry-stone walls are there but it all seems so much greener. Cacti grows freely and occasional clutches of olive trees are spattered about. Between the hills, wide valleys chop through the countryside down to the sea. One such valley, the San Blas Valley, leads down to the San Blas Bay where there is a charming, if small, sandy beach. The road towards it ends at the top of the cliff that is above the beach, and bathers have to walk the rest of the way, through terraced fields and orchards. It is a steep climb down and, of course, back up again.

The road north-west out of Nadur leads through the Ramla Valley. This is a very attractive, fertile valley, made so by the stream that used to flow down its length, and it is rich with carobs, capers and prickly pears. Cane grows wild here and locals use this long and pliable plant to build wind breaks; or alternatively, for perfect fishing rods. Most visitors though, do not travel through this valley for the flora; they come for the wide scimitar of sand that is **Ir-Ramla Beach**, one of the best beaches on Gozo.

A Roman villa used to stand on this beach, its baths nourished by the Ramla Valley stream, but today only a few stones remain. What

Ir-Ramla Beach, the best bathing spot on Gozo

can be seen, however (although it takes some finding!), is the *fougasse*. This was a very primitive gun, consisting of a large boulder with a natural cavity in it, rather like a gun barrel but closed at one end. During the early days of the Knights rule, when the Turks found Ramla beach a convenient landing spot for their regular raids, this cavity would be filled with gunpowder and grapeshot and then fired in the normal manner. As one may imagine, it was not particularly accurate. Positioned among the rocks at the eastern side of the beach, the *fougasse* is best viewed from the sea.

Calypso's Cave, said to have been the abode of the beautiful and alluring goddess, is on a cliff above Ramla Bay but one has to make a long detour around the valley to reach it. The cave itself is nothing special, little more than a hole in the ground, and those in search of naked nymphs would do better to stay on Ramla beach. Nevertheless, the view of Ramla Bay from the cave's entrance is tremendous. Note the black mark on the sea bed that can be clearly seen through the bay's blue waters. This is the remains of an underwater wall, built up to the water level by the Knights of St John, to prevent corsairs from beaching their ships.

From Calypso's Cave, cut back inland to the village of **Xaghra**. Here in the streets near the church, signs point the way to Xerri's Grotto and Ninu's Cave, underground caverns with unremarkable stalagmite and stalactite formations. Those short of time though, may want to by-pass the grottoes in favour of one of Gozo's most fascinating sights, which stands but a short distance away; the prehistoric temples of **Ggantija**.

The Maltese archipelago has some fine prehistoric sites but Ggantija is considered by many to be the best of them all. The roofs of its temples have long since collapsed but otherwise, they stand pretty much as they would have done some 5,800 years ago, when they were first constructed. So important are they historically, that their name has been given to an entire era in the development of prehistoric man on Malta— the Ggantija Phase.

The complex consists of two temples and stands on a man-made plateau on top of a hill. The stone for the temples, coralline limestone for the exterior and globigerina limestone for the interior, was quarried from the hill opposite and it must have been a tremendous feat of engineering to shift from there the huge blocks of stone that the temples are constructed from. The builders efforts seem even more impressive when one considers that the temples were actually built to a height of 6m (20ft) rather than their 2m (7ft) height today, meaning that nearly three times as much stone was originally needed. A clue to the method used to transport the stones lies at the entrance to the temples; here there are circular stones, like large cannonballs, that were presumably used as rollers.

The temples stand side by side. Together, their two façades curve outwards as if to embrace the visitor or more likely, the visitors sacrificial offerings. Offerings clearly paid a large part in the worship of the deity these temples were erected in honour of. To the left of the façades, niches have been cut into the walls. It is believed that animals would be sacrificed in these niches before being offered to the priest, who would stand at the entrance.

Facing the façade, the temple to the left is the older and the larger of the two. Passing through its entrance, one can see a primitive wash basin, perhaps used for ceremonial washing by the priest and, just inside, two libation holes drilled into the ground where the blood of the slaughtered animals would have been poured. Holes have also been drilled into the portals either side of the entrance; these are hinge holes, used to support the heavy door or curtain that would have sealed the public off from the priests inside. Through the entrance is the first, or outer, temple. This consists of two apses, one to the left, the other to the right. Stone blocks in the right-hand apse bear faint examples of the horned spiral engravings that can be seen at Tarxien, indicating that the blocks were a later addition to the temple. 'Pittings' can also be seen, small pockmarks in the surfaces of the stones, used by the builders for decoration.

The inner temple, linked to the first by a short corridor, has three apses. The right hand apse contains a small, circular hearth used to burn offerings; the left hand apse, marked by a stone platform, was used for the worship of fertility. Here in the apse's centre, a huge triangular stone was placed upside down opposite a large phallic symbol (now in the archaeological museum in Valletta). The third, central apse is empty.

The second temple was built approximately 200 years after the first and is very similar in design, except that the central apse in the inner temple is smaller. It is rather better built than the first temple though, as can be seen in the superior quality of the steps leading up to the entrance. Yet to fully appreciate the mastery of the engineers who constructed these temples, go around to the rear of the complex and examine the walls. The blocks of stones that have been used here are truly gargantuan, some weighing up to 20 tons. They were dragged here from the hill across the valley by man and animal and then toppled into place by the slow, cumbersome method of building earth ramps. The stones have been positioned in the standard 'T'-fashion, with vertical supporting slabs at regular intervals, topped by a row of smaller, rectangular blocks.

The bleached and ancient stones of the Ggantija Temples

The Ggantija Temples, one of the prehistoric marvels of Malta

Enjoying sun and sand at Marsalforn

Boats moored in the harbour at Marsalforn

After this investigation into the prehistory of Gozo, a cooling swim may be in order if this is the case head north from Xaghra and then fork left to **Marsalforn**, the one-time fishing village that is now billed as Gozo's premier beach resort. This epithet can be misleading: Marsalforn may well be 'premier' in Gozitan terms but Costa del Sol it most certainly is not. There is a night-club or two, and a fair smattering of souvenir shops, restaurants and bars, but as with most of Gozo's concessions to tourism, the emphasis is on the modest. It is a pretty village; the beach is small but inviting and next to it is the harbour, where *luzzi* are lined up colourfully in a row. In summer, it is sometimes possible to take a passenger boat from here to Valletta.

From Marsalforn, **Victoria** is 4 miles (6km) away, reached via a road that runs parallel to the verdant Marsalforn Valley. Roughly half-way along this valley, standing out sharply amidst the other, flat-topped hills, is a hill with a conical peak topped with a statue. Those looking closely will see that it is a statue of Christ. The reason for this is that in past times, this pointed peak had concerned Gozitans; they feared it was a volcano, just waiting to erupt and engulf their island. With Christ on top of the 'volcano' though, they reasoned that it would dare not erupt and as yet, it has not, although this may have more to do with the Maltese islands not being volcanic than with divine intervention. Past this hill, the road climbs steadily upwards, with the walls of the Citadel of Victoria in full view, before entering the suburbs of Gozo's capital.

Britain has left its mark on Malta in many ways — from red pillar boxes to brown beer — but in only one instance did the colonisers actually Anglicise the name of a city. That was in 1897 when the British Governor, perhaps seeking to curry favour at home, directed that Gozo's capital Rabat should henceforth be known as Victoria, so as to honour the diamond jubilee of Britain's longest serving monarch. Officially the new name has stuck, through de-colonisation and independence, but Gozitans overwhelmingly still refer to it by the old which means, quite simply, 'the city'.

There are strong similarities between Victoria and the one-time capital of Malta, Mdina. Like Mdina, Victoria has a Citadel that stands high on a hill commanding its surrounds, its solid walls clearly visible from afar; like Mdina, it began its existence as a fortified Bronze Age settlement and has been continually inhabited ever since; and like Mdina, it exudes a leisurely, almost other-worldly charm that effortlessly infects its visitors.

Coming from Marsalforn, one enters Victoria on Capuchins Street. This ends at the city's main thoroughfare, officially called Republic Street but more commonly known by its old name, Racecourse

Street. The source of the original name will be abundantly clear to anyone who visits Victoria for the *festas* of the Virgin Mary and of St George. On these days the street resonates to the thunder of hooves as local men, perched precariously atop their sturdy mounts, compete furiously in mule and donkey races.

Turn right into Republic Street, pass the main post office and enter Independence Square, another new place name rarely used by Victorians-cum-Rabatians who call it by the name it bore for centuries, It-Tokk or 'the meeting place'. There is a cloth and clothing market here every weekday morning, when the square heaves with shoppers, but as with elsewhere on the Maltese archipelago it quietens down for the afternoon siesta before livening again in the evening. Sight-wise, there is little of interest here; for something to 'see' one must walk a few minutes south into the old town, to St George's Square where there is the seventeenth-century **Church of St George**. With an interior recently re-modelled in neo-Baroque, it contains a remarkable statue of the saint himself, as well as some fine wall paintings, particularly within the dome. The area around St Georges makes for pleasant meandering; plenty of bars and shops secreted away in narrow, shady, atmospheric streets.

It is the **Citadel** though, that is the main attraction of Victoria. This, a town within a fortress, is easy to reach: just make the easy ascent up from It-Tokk to the city gates, positioned between two huge demi-bastions in a fortification style typical of the Knights of St John. There are in fact two gates here, located side by side, although the first one, the larger of the two, is a rather crude affair. This gate is a relatively recent creation, opened so that participants in the *festa* of Santa Maria could comfortably flood out from the Cathedral within the Citadel and enter the city proper without having to squeeze painfully through the smaller, original gate, which stands to the right. As is to be expected, this gate is the more interesting of the two; half-way through, a prayer niche dedicated to the Virgin and to St Anne has been carved and at its end, at eye-level, a stone block has been inserted that bears distinctive Latin inscriptions. Dating from the second century and the Roman occupation of Malta, this was once the pedestal of a statue that stood at the entrance to the city and its script shows that even then, Victoria was the capital of the Gozo municipality.

Once inside, the Citadel's convoluted street lay-out renders pointless any attempt to give meaningful directions. Visitors, however, need have no fear of missing anything worthwhile: the area to be covered is very small and all streets and places of interest are clearly marked. Accordingly, what follows below is a listing of what can be

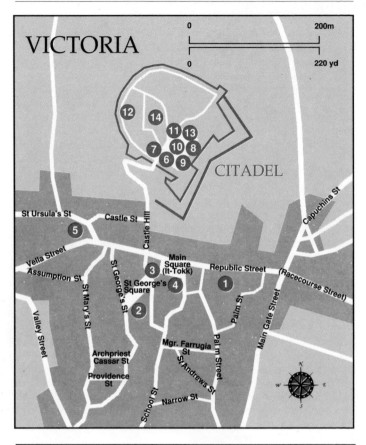

VICTORIA

1 Main Post Office
2 Church of St George
3 Information Office
4 Cloth and Clothing Market (weekdays)
5 Jewellery Market (Sunday morning)

CITADEL

6 Bondi Palace (Archaeological Museum)
7 Old Law Courts
8 Archbishop's Palace
9 Govenor's Palace
10 Cathedral of Santa Maria
11 Cathedral Museum
12 Armoury
13 Natural Science Museum
14 Folklore Museum

found within the Citadel, with directions and/or landmarks given where possible. Incidentally, the Citadel's serpentine street plan is no historical accident: the city was designed this way and for three reasons. Firstly, so that attackers would have difficulty orienting themselves; secondly, for the shade that is provided by tall buildings flanking narrow streets; and thirdly, to facilitate better wind currents, so that the city could be kept cooler still.

The first sight of interest is easy enough to find, being immediately to the right as one enters the Citadel through the original gate. This is the **Bondi Palace**, once the home of a prominent city family and the residence of the hated Grand Inquisitor, chief of the Inquisition, whenever he was in town. Today, this sumptuous building serves as an with artefacts that range from the stone phallus that once adorned the Ggantija temple to amphorae that were recovered from the wreck

A prayer niche within the main gate of the Citadel, Victoria

of a Roman galley that sank off the coast near Xlendi. Of particular interest is the display of Phoenician amulets; note their distinctive 'Eye of Osiris' design, still reproduced today by Maltese sailors on the bows of their *luzzi*, so that the boat may 'see' any potential dangers, and be ready to avoid them.

Yet it is to Market Square that most visitors gravitate upon arriving in the Citadel. Here one can find the old law courts, the archbishops palace, and the Governors palace, all fine structures but all of which pale into insignificance when measured against the edifice that dominates the square, the seventeenth-century **Cathedral of Santa Maria**, the Virgin Mary. So often Baroque churches can seem over-blown and ostentatious; this is not one of them.

Externally the cathedral is quite plain, although exquisitely pro-portioned, and is best appreciated from inside. The floor is a colour-ful spangle of tombstones, the walls plastered in paintings and the ceiling drips with two long rows of crystal chandeliers. The altar is bedecked in silver and there are intricate statues of Christ and of the Virgin. The dome is a revelation, painted with fine delicacy. Yet take a closer look at the dome, and the true genius of the painter becomes apparent. For this is not a dome at all. It is a phoney, the flat ceiling having been painted merely to represent one and the effect succeeds, superbly. Near the cathedral is the Cathedral Museum, home to the usual collection of vestments, motifs, ex-votos and so on.

The Citadel has several other museums. The **Armoury** is very small, just a single room opening out onto the street and sealed off by an iron grille through which one can view amongst other things suits of armour, swords and shields. It is opposite the **Natural Science Museum**, also small but with informative displays on subjects such as the geological composition of Gozo. The **Folklore Museum** is larger, and is well worth a visit. Found in a beautiful old house (note the dual-arched windows, dating from Norman times), its artefacts complement their setting delightfully. Downstairs there are old scales and pots and scythes and ploughs, even an old corn grinder, while upstairs each room is devoted to a different theme such as hunting, fishing, religion, fireworks and *festas*. The museum is on Bernardo de Opuo Street, which is named after a soldier of the Knights who, during a Turkish raid in 1579, died fighting having first slain his wife and two daughters rather than let them be carried off into slavery by the bandits. Lastly, one can ascend the battlements, to the highest point on Gozo, and enjoy the vista over this now quiet and soothing island.

The Citadel is short on restaurants and bars but those seeking to satiate the body as well as the mind could do worse than try the Cittadella Restaurant, where one can get a good meal in relaxed surroundings. For just a drink and a snack, then the tea-room on top of St Martin's Cavalier on the battlements is a good choice; and for just a drink, there is the Imbid Tar-Razzett shop on Fosse Street, near the city gates. Sandwiched between souvenir shops, this establishment sells Gozitan wines produced on the owners own farm. The wine may not appeal to all — it has a very woody aftertaste, not unlike Greek *retsina* — but as there are plenty of free samples on offer, finding something to suit should not be a problem. The shop also sells *Tamakari*, the traditional Maltese liqueur.

To continue the tour of Gozo from Victoria, head south out of the city on the road marked 'Xlendi'. The route passes through the Victorian suburb of Fontana, one of the few places on the Maltese islands to have an Italian, rather than an Arabic, name. In Italian *fontana* means 'fountain' and there are two of them here, both once having formed part of a public bath-house built by the Knights. At the end of this road is the sea and **Xlendi**, a quiet and scenic village nestling comfortably at the end of a deep creek, hemmed in by lofty cliffs. The sea is astonishingly clear here, wonderful for swimmers, and it is little wonder that Xlendi becomes more and more popular as each year passes, particularly amongst the yachting fraternity who find the sheltered creek the perfect anchorage. Yet as with Marsalforn, the village is barely developed at all when judged by the standards of other Mediterranean resorts and for those who seek to 'get away from it all', but who still wish to retain a modicum of comfort, Xlendi could well be the place. It has the added attraction of possessing several good restaurants; particularly delectable is the fresh fish served at Ic-Cima Restaurant on St Simeon's Street, above the town overlooking the creek.

Those who wish to explore this area can make the lovely one mile walk west along the cliff tops to **Wardija Point**, where one can find the excavated remains of a Roman sanctuary, including an oblong chamber filled with wall niches. Few people visit this lonely and dramatic site, where one can feel like the only living being on the island.

Once in Xlendi, there is only one road back out again, that which returns to Victoria. So, back in the capital, take the westward road that is signposted 'San Lawrenz'. This road passes under an aqueduct built by the British at a point where a right fork takes one, via the village of Ghasri, to **Zebbug**, a lethargic little village that somehow seems to have become lost in time. Take a look at the painting of the Madonna in the left transept of the parish church here, and if her face is unduly pale, then worry: tradition says that this portents some terrible disaster is pending for Malta. Continuing on past the aque-

The Azure Window, one of the geological wonders at Dwejra Point

Fungus Rock, once zealously guarded by the Knights of St John

duct though, one reaches another junction, where a fork north leads to the island's holiest site, the grand church of Ta' Pinu.

Ta' Pinu Church may look as if it was built only fifty-odd years ago — indeed, the present Romanesque building was — but its contemporary exterior conceals a long and remarkable history. The original chapel here was built simply from stone in the sixteenth century, and was dedicated to the Assumption of Our Lady, but within decades fell into disrepair and disuse. Then, in the 1670's, it came under the care of one Pinu Gauci, a devout and wealthy man who restored the chapel and brought it back into service. From then on, and in typical Maltese fashion, the church became known as Ta' Pinu, quite literally, Pinu's. Roughly two centuries later, on the 22 June 1883, a 45-year-old spinster named Karmela Grima was returning home from work in the fields near Ta' Pinu. As she neared the chapel she heard an ethereal voice calling her, commanding her to go inside at once and to say three Hail Marys. Overawed, the woman did and although she was only ever to tell one other person of her experience, a relative who also claimed to have heard the voice, the news soon spread. At first, only locals came to the church, to pray for miracles of healing, but as more and more of these prayers were answered, pilgrims flocked to Ta' Pinu from afar. So famous became the chapel, that the church authorities decided to build another church around and over the original. This allows Pinu's chapel to remain within the new church, its altar dripping with ex-votos and motifs left by the

The festa *is as much for children as for adults*

thousands of pilgrims who have knelt there in faith.

Karmela Grima lived in the nearby village of **Gharb** and her small house there has now been converted into a museum, telling the story in words and photographs of the miraculous chapel of Ta' Pinu. The area around the village incidentally, is fine for wild, lovely, lonely walks.

Back on the road to San Lawrenz two shopping stops can be made. The first is at the **Gozo Glass Factory**, where artisans blow great balloons of glass in the time-honoured fashion; the second is at the Ta' Dbeigi Crafts Village. Located within an old army barracks, this is full of shops selling all manner of Maltese souvenirs — knitwear, filigree, lace and so on — at standard prices. **San Lawrenz** itself is a pretty enough village, but there is little to actually see. The village was for many years the home of Nicholas Monsarrat, author of a book that should be required reading for any visitor to the Maltese islands, *The Kappillan of Malta*.

West of San Lawrenz, the earth seems to fall away as the road descends in a rush to what for many visitors is the most gorgeous spot on Gozo, Dwejra Point. The route there is striking, the road passing between two valleys cut millennia before by streams that have long since ceased to flow. Development is sparse, human habitation sparser still and the whole impression is of a land far larger than this diminutive island. As the Mediterranean draws nearer, the two valleys converge and the road runs out, near a small chapel that overlooks the first of the two geological wonders of **Dwejra Point**, the Inland Sea.

The **Inland Sea** lies at the bottom of a large natural bowl, sealed off from the sea by a sheer and precipitous cliff. It is however, not quite the perfect lake it first appears to be: at its far end, the water has bored a hole in the base of the cliff, creating a tunnel that links it to the open sea. There is even a beach on its shores, albeit one small and pebbly. Avoid any temptation to swim or jump off the rock jetties near the beach; the water there is far to shallow for a safe 'splash'. Besides, these jetties are very slippery.

The second geological oddity of Dwejra Point is a short clamber over rocks away. This, one of the most photographed sights on Gozo, is the **Azure Window**, an immense rectangular rock protruding into the sea breached by a large hole in its centre, created by the waves of centuries crashing against it. The result is this 'window' effect. The 'azure' comes from the colour of the sea around the rock, as clear a blue as one could possibly imagine. The whole area is perfect for divers but those who lack an aqualung can still enjoy the waters; there are plenty of rocks to swim off.

Dwejra Point was a place held dear by the Knights of St John, not so much for its beauty (although presumably, they enjoyed that too) as for the fact that offshore stands the great stony hulk that is **Fungus Rock**. All other duties aside, the Knights were primarily hospitallers whose medicines were most often extracted from flora, and on this rock grew a plant they called *Fungus Gaulitanus*. This leafless, parasitic plant, purple and red in colour, could be used for curing ulcers and other intestinal complaints but was extremely rare. For this reason, the Knights built a watchtower overlooking the rock to ensure that no one picked the plant without permission — indeed, to do so was to commit an offence punishable by galley servitude. So prized was this plant that Grandmasters would often present it to visiting royalty and dignitaries during the ritual exchange of gifts. It was a General of the Knights galleys who first discovered this plant and its healing properties; accordingly, Fungus Rock is sometimes referred to as *Il-Gebla tal General*, the 'Rock of the General'.

The road back to Mgarr travels through Victoria where one can head south once more, via Munxar (the road passes the remains of a small prehistoric temple) to **Sannat**, another village where the local lace-makers enjoy a fine reputation. Beyond Sannat is **Ta'Cenc**, standing atop cliffs that plunge vertically hundreds of feet down to the sea. Here one is once again walking in the footsteps of neolithic man for nearby are prehistoric dolmens and some good examples of cart ruts etched deeply into the rocky landscape. A wonderful walk from here is down a twisting cliffside path to **Mgarr ix-Xini**, a picturesque little inlet as yet discovered by only a few. The oldest building in Ta'Cenc is the manor house, since converted into a luxurious five-star hotel.

North of Sannat, the road reaches the main Victoria-Mgarr route which, if one turns towards Mgarr, takes one through the village of **Xewkija** where there is one last marvel to be enjoyed. It takes no genius to note that the Maltese are intensely proud of their churches and this, combined with a rich streak of Mediterranean excess, has resulted in a church that has a supported dome which is the third largest in size in Europe only St Peter's in Rome and St Paul's in London being larger. Why Xewkija needs such an immense religious edifice to rival such great cities may be open to question — the church's capacity is three times more than that of the population of the village itself — but trifling matters such as that do not bother the villagers who paid for its construction themselves.

✳ Comino

For an island that measures not much more than a mile in any direction, and which has a permanent population of only three, there is a lot happening on Comino. This is thanks primarily to the two hotels that have been built here, whose owners have done their best to exploit all that the island has to offer. Some of the finest bathing on the Maltese archipelago is to be had here, yet Comino is filled with a sense of peace and solitude that can almost makes one feel marooned, as if on an unknown desert island, a million miles from anywhere. In actuality, of course, visitors to Comino are nowhere near marooned. Gozo is to the west, Malta to the east and boats operated by the hotels link all three, eight times a day.

Comino (the island draws its name from the spice cumin, which was grown here during Roman times) barely features in Malta's history. Pirates once used it as a base for attacking trading ships passing between Gozo and Malta: indeed, their presence became so pestilential that the Knights of St John built the still-standing St Mary's Tower on the island's highest point, to keep the bandits away. In time, a small village grew up around the tower although today it is all but deserted, only an old woman and her two nephews remaining out of a populace that was once 100 strong. The reason for this exodus can be seen in the landscape of Comino; the island is very barren, with only parched, low-lying vegetation. Water in particular, is very scarce and Comino's hotels have had to construct their own reverse osmosis plants, converting sea water into fresh, in order to meet their own needs.

The two hotels of Comino, the Comino and the Nautical, are both owned by a Swiss company. They stand at the north-eastern edge of the island a ten-minute walk from each other, the Comino occupying St Mary's Bay and the Nautical, St Nicholas's Bay, each one having been built next to one of the island's two small beaches. Note, however, that these beaches are privately owned by the hotels and non-residents who wish to enjoy them, and the range of water sports that each one offers, have to contact the hotels in advance and book in as day members, at a cost that includes lunch. Attached to, but not owned by, the hotels is a private diving school which welcomes both beginners and the experienced. Comino is particularly good for divers: the waters around the island are so clear as to be almost transparent, and the heavily indented coastline is filled with tiny coves and underwater caves.

Yet the best-loved bathing spot on Comino is unquestionably the **Blue Lagoon**, a five minute stroll south from St Nicholas's Bay.

The sheer cliffs of the Comino coastline

Comino is a haven of quiet and calm

Despite its name, this is not a lagoon in the purest sense, being not totally enclosed by land, but hemmed in by a ring of small islets, the largest of which is Cominetto. The clear blueness of its waters, however, is indisputablewhich is the reason why it has become extremely popular as a day trip excursion from Malta and Gozo.

Additional Information

Places to Visit

Ggantija Temples
Near Xaghra
☎ 553194
Open: 1 October to 31 March 8.30am-4.30pm Monday to Saturday. 1 April to 15 June and 16-30 September 8.30am-6.30pm Monday to Saturday. 16 June to 15 September 8.30am-7pm. Sundays 8.30am-3pm. Closed public holidays.

Ghajnsielem
Gozo Heritage
Mgarr Road
☎ 551475
Open: daily 9am-5pm.

Gharb
KarmelaGrima Museum
Open: 1 October to 30 June 1-4pm Sundays only. 1 July to 30 September 11am-4pm daily.

Gozo Glass Factory
Gharb-San Lawrenz Crossroads
Open: 9am-7pm Monday to Saturday.

San Lawrenz
Ta Dbiegi Crafts Village
Open: 11.30am-3.30pm Monday to Saturday.

Victoria
Natural Science Museum
Quarters Street
☎ 556153
Open: 1 October to 31 March 8.30am-4.30pm Monday to Saturday. 1 April to 15 June and 16 September to 30 September 8.30am-6.30pm Monday to Saturday. 16 June to 15 September 8.30am-7pm. Sundays 8.30am-3pm.

Folklore Museum
Bernardo de Opuo Street
Citadel
☎ 556144
Open: 1 October to 31 March 8.30am-4.30pm Monday to Saturday. 1 April to 15 June and 16-30 September 8.30am-6.30pm Monday to Saturday. 16 June 15 September 8.30am-7pm. Sundays 8.30am-3pm.

Archaeology Museum
Prisons Street
Citadel
☎ 556144
Open: 1 October to 31 March 8.30am-4.30pm Monday to Saturday. 1 April to 15 June and 16 to 30 September 8.30am-6.30pm Monday to Saturday. 16 June to 15 September 8.30am-7pm. Sundays 8.30am-3pm. Closed public holidays.

Armoury
Quarters Street
Citadel
☎ 455951
Open: 1 October to 31 March
8.30am-4.30pm Monday to
Saturday. 1 April to 15 June and 16
to 30 September 8.30am-6.30pm
Monday to Saturday. 16 June to 15
September 8.30am-7pm. Sundays
8.30am-3pm. Closed public holidays.

Cathedral Museum
Citadel
Open: 10.30am-4.30pm Monday to
Saturday. Closed Sundays and
public holidays.
Imbid Tar-Razzett
4 Fosse Street
Citadel
Open: Monday to Saturday 9am-5pm.

Useful Information

Restaurant

Xlendi
Ic-Cima Restaurant
St Simon Street
☎ 558407
General Post Office
Republic Street
Victoria
Open: 8am-10pm daily, but to only
9pm on Sundays.

Emergency Numbers
Police
Gozo 562040
Comino 573960

Ambulance 199
Traffic Accidents 562040//562044
General Hospital: 561600

Travel
Heliport 557905/561301
Gozo Channel Ferry Company
Mgarr Harbour 556114/556743

Tourist Information Centres

Victoria
Palm Street
☎ 556554
Open: Monday to Saturday
8.30am-12.30pm and 1.15-6pm.
Sundays 8.30am-1pm. Public
holidays 8.30am-1pm and 3-6pm.

Mgarr Harbour
☎ 553343
Open: Monday to Saturday
8.30am-12.30pm and 1.15-6pm.
Sundays 8.30am-1pm. Public
holidays 8.30am-1pm and 3-6pm.

Malta: Fact File

Accommodation

Malta is a small island where space to build hotels is limited and during the height of summer the number of beds available on the island are not always plentiful enough to meet demand. This is particularly true during the *ferro Augusto*, the Italian industrial holiday which falls during the first two weeks of August and when half the population of Italy seems to have temporarily emigrated to the island. The upshot of all this is that those who intend to travel to Malta in either July or August are strongly advised to book their accommodation in advance. Outside of July and August, however, the visitor should have few problems arranging a place to stay on the spot although they can make this process easier by contacting the Maltese tourist office in their home country and asking for a list of the accommodation available on the island. Malta has a wide selection of accommodation, with prices to suit every pocket. One can stay in either hotels, guest houses, self-catering apartments or luxurious holiday complexes although the latter two options are often pre-booked way in advance.

Hotels on Malta are classified according to the standard 'star' system, with one star being the most basic and five star the most deluxe. As with any country, you tend to get what you are prepared to pay for but at least here visitors can be sure that every establishment is regularly checked by government inspectors to ensure that standards are being maintained and that each hotel is deserving of its star rating. All hotels quote prices that include breakfast.

Although all rooms in one-star hotels will have a wash basin, none will have a private bathroom and desk service may not always be available. Likewise, many of the two-star hotels have only common bath and toilet facilities, although some will have rooms that are en suite. There should, however, be a telephone in the room. A three-star hotel will not only have rooms with private bath and telephone, but will also offer extras such as laundry, dry cleaning, a bar and a restaurant whereas with a four-star, one enters the realms of opulence, with all the facilities of a three-star plus air conditioning, a swimming pool, room service, a lounge and a hairdresser. For a hotel that offers spacious, air-conditioned rooms with television and radio, as well as 24-hour room service, sports facilities, a nightclub, a swimming pool and other such luxuries, stay in a five-star.

Budget travellers can make use of Malta's privately owned guest houses which, while being basic, are often cosy and comfortable and a good place in which to meet fellow itinerants. These establishments have few frills about them: bathroom and toilet facilities will almost certainly be shared and there may not even be a telephone available, let alone one in the room. Note that Valletta's guest houses sometimes suffer chronically from water problems: ie, the supply may be cut off for hours at a time.

The vast bulk of places to stay can be found along the island's northern coast, particularly in the following areas: Sliema, St Julian's, Paceville, St George's, St Paul's and Mellieha. Here the visitor is well catered for, with plenty of restaurants, bars, water sport activities, nightclubs, souvenir shops and so on. On the down side, these areas can also appear noisy, brash and for many, over-populated with tourists. Yet the visitor has options other than those offered along the Sliema-Mellieha stretch. Lovers of history may want to consider staying in either Valletta or Rabat, or even Mdina, which despite its diminutive size, has a hotel, the Xara Palace. Those who want or need to be near a sandy beach can stay at the Golden Sands Hotel at Golden Bay, or at Marsaxlokk while those with the desire to immerse themselves in the quiet life of the Maltese interior can do so in some of the larger villages and towns, such as Attard and Balzan.

Gozo too has a wide selection of available accommodation, most of it around the resort of Marsalforn but also in Victoria, Mgarr, Xlendi and Sannat, where there is the de luxe Ta Cenc Hotel, built around an old manor house. There are two hotels on Comino, the Comino and the Nautical, both operated by the same company. There are no campsites on Malta, and pitching a tent freelance is strongly frowned upon, partly due to the risk of fire.

A list of accommodation can be obtained from all tourist offices on Malta.

Climate

Typically Mediterranean, Malta has a fine, healthy climate. Brief and mild winters give way in late April to summers that stretch through to early October, a time of year when rainfall is virtually unknown, when ten hours of sunshine can be expected every day and when the average daily temperature is a glowing 32°C (90°F). July and August are the hottest months although the weather is seldom unbearably warm, thanks to cooling sea breezes. Occasionally, however, the *xlokk* blows in from Saharan Africa, a hot and muggy wind that sucks all the fresh air upwards out of reach, turns the atmosphere heavy and oppressive, and makes even a short stroll seem the most arduous struggle. Summer is always followed by what the Maltese call 'Saint Martin's summer', lasting from late September to early November, when bright and clear spells are interspersed with gentle, refreshing showers.

An average of only 58cm (23in) of rain falls on Malta each year, mostly between late November and early March. January is the wettest month, with short but often violent rain storms, but there is never any snow and rarely any frost. Indeed, even in winter the sun is out for an average of six hours daily and the average temperature is a comfortable 14°C (58°F).

See page 162 for climate graph.

Culture

Cultural life in Valletta revolves around the Manoel Theatre, built during the reign of Grandmaster Manoel de Vilhena and the oldest functioning theatre in Europe outside Great Britain. The performances shown here, both in English and Malti (it is worth checking what language any particular performance is in before booking a seat) are of a high quality and are pleasingly varied in scope. A typical months schedule could include an opera, a couple of plays, music by the Manoel Theatre Orchestra and a piano recital. One may even be lucky enough to see an international star perform — Yehudi Menuhin, Segovia and the Bolshoi Ballet are amongst those who have trod the theatre's boards. Ticket prices are, as a rule, much lower than those for equivilant shows in Northern Europe or America. The theatre publishes a monthly pamphlet advertising what is on which is available from the tourist office and good hotels. Alternatively, ☎ 222618/ 222659.

Maltese art is not particularly well known but can still be impressive. Major galleries on the archipelago include Galerie 100 in St Julian's and Galea's Art in Valletta. For the cream of Maltese art from past and present though, visit the Museum of Fine Arts in Valletta where there are some truly superb *objects d'art* on display. For more information about the museum, consult the Valletta chapter within this book.

Those for whom appreciating the finer points of Maltese theatre and art is not their idea of the perfect vacation need not be disappointed. Malta has a thriving nightlife, most of it concentrated in Sliema, St Paul's, St Julian's and Paceville on the northern coast. Bars, which open at 9am, do not tend to close until 1am and in the nightclubs, the party goes on until 4am. Open air disco's, such as Beachaven on Xemxija Hill at St Paul's Bay are growing in popularity. Note that many hotel bars are closed for *siesta* between 1am and 4pm.

Gamblers will be pleased to learn that, although it is illegal for the Maltese, a flutter can be enjoyed at the luxurious Dragonera Palace Hotel in St Julian's (☎ 344550-2) where roulette, baccarat, black jack and *boule* can be played, international rules applying. Winnings can be spent in the opulent Marquis , the casino's restaurant. Films in Maltese are shown in their original language. There are several cinemas on the island, including:

Embassy Cinema	Alhambra Cinema
St Lucia Street	Tower Road
Valletta	Sliema
☎ 245991	☎ 313463

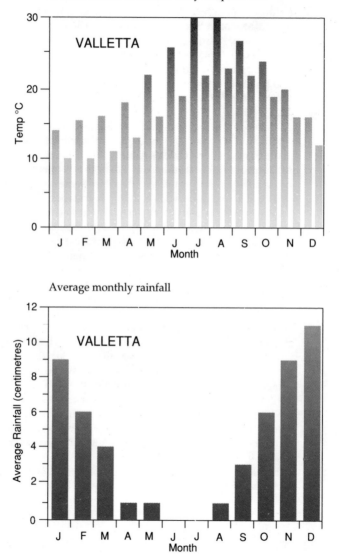

Maximum and minimum daily temperatures

VALLETTA

Average monthly rainfall

VALLETTA

Currency and Credit Cards

Malta's unit of currency is the *Lira* (LM) which is divided into 100 cents. Notes come in denominations of LM 20, 10, 5 and 2 and coins in LM 1 and 50, 20, 10, 5, 2 and 1 cents. Note for note, the Maltese *lira* is worth more than the British pound. For British visitors, this can take some getting used to.

Changing money is an easy process and even those arriving in Malta in the middle of the night can soon arm themselves with some local *lira*, thanks to the 24 hour change facilities at Luqa airport. Travellers cheques can be exchanged at banks, post offices, the better hotels and can be used instead of cash at many shops, restaurants and car rental companies although it is always worth confirming that this is the case before, for example, one eats. Eurocheques can be cashed at banks and the major credit cards — ie: Access/ Mastercard, Visa, Diners Club and American Express — are all widely accepted. Banking hours are 8.30am-12.30pm Monday to Thursday, 4-7pm Friday and 8.30am-12noon Saturdays. All banks close on Sundays and public holidays.

Malta is not a particularly expensive country, but neither is it exceptionally cheap and a good general rule for vacationers is to bring as much money to Malta as they would expect to spend on a similar holiday in their home country.

Disabled Travellers

Malta is not the easiest of countries for the disabled traveller, although neither is it the most difficult. On the up side most of the prehistoric sites can be visited by the wheelchair bound without too much difficulty (with the exceptions of the Hypogeum and Ghar Dalam), as can places such as the San Anton Gardens and the majority of towns and villages. On the downside the narrow and stepped streets of cities such as Valletta, Mdina and Victoria are difficult to negotiate, and churches and cathedrals can pose a problem too, most of them having a series of steps leading up to the main entrance. Overall though, there is a distinct lack of even the most simple of facilities: ramps for example, and specially designed hotel rooms. Nevertheless, things are changing for the better and there is a growing awareness within the

Maltese tourist industry of the needs of the disabled. Luqa airport for example, is wheelchair friendly. Wheelchairs may be hired in Malta, merely by writing to one of the following addresses below prior to arrival. Be sure to ask for a letter of confirmation stating that a wheelchair will be available.

St Luke's Hospital
Administration Division
Guardamangia
Malta

The Administration Secretary
Rehabilitation Centre for the Physically Handicapped
Kordin
Paola
Malta

In the case of St Luke's Hospital, wheelchairs can also be hired on arrival upon presentation of a medical certificate. Disabled people wishing to drive in Malta should apply for a special 'disabled' badge which is placed on the car's windscreen and which entitles the bearer to park in areas (within reason) where parking is otherwise forbidden. To apply for the badge, contact:

Centru Hidma Socjali
Santa Venera
Malta
☎ 446 007 or 441 313

For any further information, contact the nearest office of the National Tourism Organisation.

Dress Regulations

Visitors should dress and act appropriately while in a church — ie: to behave in a quiet, decorous fashion and to dress modestly, with legs and arms fully covered.

Note that topless bathing is not permitted on Malta and that strolling around town in a skimpy bikini is more likely to arouse looks of contempt than of admiration.

Electricity

Those travelling from Britain need not bring electricity converters. Malta uses the square-fitting three-pin British plugs and sockets, running off a 240 volt, single phase 50 cycle electricity supply.

Embassies and High Commissions

The main Maltese Embassies and High Commissions are:

Australia and New Zealand
261 La Perouse Street
Red Hill
Canberra ACT 2063
☎ (062) 951 586

Canada
Hon Consul General
PO Box 186 STC 'C'
Crosbie Buildings
Crosbie Road
St Johns
Newfoundland AIC 5J2
☎ (709) 722 2744

Commercial Counsellor and
Hon Consul General
1 St John's Road
Suite 305
Toronto
Ontario M6P 4C7
☎ (416) 767 4902/2901

UK
Malta High Commission
16 Kensington Square
London W8 5HH
☎ (071) 938 1712

USA
Permanent Mission of Malta
to the United Nation
249 East 35th Street
New York NY 10016
☎ (212) 725 2345

Embassy of Malta
2017 Connecticut Avenue
Washington DC 20008
☎ (202) 462 3611

Irish Republic
Hon Consul
Traverslea Glengeary Co
Dublin
☎ (1) 801 081

Embassies and High Commissions in Malta are:
Australia
Australian High Commission
Airways House
Gaiety Land
PO Box 8
Sliema
☎ 338 201

UK
British High Commission
7 St Anne Street
Floriana
☎ 233 134/8

USA
Embassy of the United States
of America
Development House
St Anne Street
Floriana
☎ 243 653/240 424/240 425

Festivals

The Festa

Every parish on Malta and Gozo has a patron saint and every year, the feast day of that saint is celebrated in that most unique of Maltese events, the *festa*. These are tremendous occasions, a riot of fireworks, bands and feasting, intermingled with Christian worship and attended by virtually every member of the host town or village. *Festas* are held nearly all year round on Malta, with several occuring every weekend during the summer and the visitor to the island should view at least one while there. No other event offers a better insight into Maltese tradition and culture.

Festas, except when held on public holidays, are normally celebrated on the first Saturday night and Sunday that follows that particular saint's feast day. Festivities normally begin at around 7.30pm or 8pm, although it is worth arriving an hour or so before, not only to get a good position in front of the church but also to soak up some of the pre-*festa* atmosphere: the streets slowly filling up with people, the general air of bustle, and the rich and fatty smell of fast food being fried by jolly street traders. Other traders sell that traditional *festa* snack, *nougat*, served from Georgian-type stalls of lavishly polished wood after having been weighed in old, gleaming scales. The streets will be splendidly decorated with brightly coloured pendants and streamers and flags and every 10m (33ft) or so along the high street, there will stand papier mache statues of the Madonna and of the saint who is about to be honoured. Slowly, the area around the steps leading up to the church begins to fill up as the service that is being held inside begins to draw to a close.

The *festa* begins proper when a procession begins to file out of the church, children and adults alike dressed in vestal garb, some carrying elaborately carved crosses in their hands. Then, fireworks explode in the sky above and the village's brass band strikes up with gusto as a heavy statue, usually carved from wood, of the saint is carried shoulder high out of the church and into the midst of the throng. The band leaves its stand to file into line behind the statue and the procession begins, marching to music through the streets of the parish to return back to the church where the partying begins, music, feasting and dancing that will last well into the early hours.

The *festa* was not always so spectacular. Originally, it was only a small, local religious festival, held to honour the saint and with food and wine provided by a local nobleman. The arrival of the Knights of St John, however, saw the *festa* take on a new significance. The Knights loved to celebrate and almost any event would become an excuse for a party and the more lavish the party, the better. One such event is still celebrated on the island, Carnival, held across Malta but particularly in Valletta during the second weekend of May, and with music, dancing and fancy dress. Accordingly, the festivals of the Order began to be combined with the more traditional *festas* of the Maltese. Fireworks became to be regularly used at the *festas*, particularly if the event was to honour those such as St Barbara, the patron saint of, among others, artillerymen. Music was introduced, initially on a modest scale, and the tradition of carrying the saint in procession began. The Knights would often contribute to the cost of a *festa* although their motives may not always have been entirely philanthropic — indeed, some historians have argued that their benevolence was merely a cheap way of stifling popular discontent by giving the populace something to look forward to, so that they could forget the miserable conditions they were living under.

The advent of British rule brought a new prosperity to the Maltese and the *festa* flourished further, incorporating with it some decidedly British customs, brass bands, for example, which since the mid-nineteenth century have been a regular feature of the *festa*. New *festas* were started, to commemorate new and great events in the Catholic calendar, such as the apparition of the Madonna at Lourdes in 1858. By this time, the *festas* were being solely organised, and paid for, by the residents of each parish, meaning that the success of a *festa* depended on the amount of time, money and effort each village was prepared to put into the event. Consequently, rivalry between the various villages grew, a rivalry that still persists today as to who can put on the best firework show, display the best decorations, and so on.

It is fair to say that the *festa* has not got the total approval of every islander. Some see its very lavishness as a denial of its original Christian motive and claim that it bears more relationship to a pagan festival than a religious ceremony. Most, however, love the occasion and today, the cult of the *festa* is as strong as ever.

DATE	FESTA	TOWN
February 10	St Paul	Valletta
Mid-March	St Gregory	Kercem, Gozo
	St Joseph	Rabat
Easter	Various *festas* at	various villages
End-April	St Joseph	Xaghra, Gozo
Early May	St Publius	Floriana
	Our Lady of the Grotto	Rabat
	St Augustine	Valletta
Mid-May	St Anthony of Padova	Birkirkara
End May	The Annunciation	Tarxien
	Our Lady of Fatima	Gwardamanga
	St Paul Munxar,	Gozo
Early June	St Joseph	Hamrun
	St Joseph	Ghaxaq
	St Joseph	Kirkop
	Corpus Christi Ghasri,	Gozo
Mid-June	St Philip	Zebbug
	Holy Trinity	Marsa
	Our Lady of Lourdes	Qrendi
	Sacred Heart of Jesus	Fontana, Gozo
End June	St Catherine	Zejtun
	Our Lady of the Lily	Mqabba
	Corpus Christi	Rabat
	St John the Baptist	Xewkija, Gozo
	St George	Qormi
	St Nicholas	Siggiewi
June 29	St Peter and St Paul	Mdina
	St Peter and St Paul	Nadur, Gozo
	St Paul	Rabat

	Immaculate Conception	Hamrun
	St Andrew	Luqa
	Our Lady of the Sacred Heart	Sliema
	St Elizabeth	Gharb, Gozo
Mid-July	Our Lady of Sokkors	Kercem, Gozo
	St Joseph	Kalkara
	Our Lady of Pompeii	Marsaxlokk
	Annunciation	Balzan
	Our Lady of Mount Carmel	Gzira
	Our Lady of Mount Carmel	Valletta
	St George	Victoria, Gozo
	St Sebastian	Qormi
	St Joseph	Msida
	Our Lady of Mount Carmel	Birkirkara
	Our Lady of Mount Carmel	Msida
End July	Our Lady of Sorrows	St Paul's Bay
	Our Lady of Mount Carmel	Zurrieq
	Christ the King	Paola
	St Margaret	Sannat, Gozo
	St Anna	Marsascala
	St Venera	St Venera
	St Joseph	Zebbug
Early August	St Peter	Birzebbuga
	St Joseph	Qala, Gozo
	Our Lady of Lourdes	San Gwan
	St Dominic	Valletta
	Transfiguration of Our Lord	Lija
	St Lawrence	Vittoriosa
	St Gejtanu	Hamrun
	St Lawrence	San Lawrenz,Gozo
15 August	The Assumption of Our Lady	various villages
End August	The Assumption of Our Lady	Dingli
	The Assumption of Our Lady	Mgarr (Malta)
	Our Lady of Lourdes	Paola
	St Helen	Birkirkara
	Stella Maria	Sliema
	The Assumption	Zebbug, Gozo
	Maria Regina	Marsa
	St Paul	Safi
	St Bartholomew	Ghargur
	Our Lady of Loreto	Ghajnsielem,Gozo
	St Julien	St Julien's
	St Dominic	Vittoriosa
Early Sept	St Catherine	Zurrieq
	St Gregory	Sliema
	Our Lady of the Cintura	Rabat

	Our Lady of Mount Carmel	Xlendi,Gozo
	The Nativity of Our Lady	Mellieha
	The Nativity of Our Lady	Senglea
	The Nativity of Our Lady	Naxxar
	The Nativity of Our Lady	Xaghra,Gozo
Mid Sept	Our Lady of Grace	Zabbar
	Our Lady of Grace	Victoria,Gozo
	St Leonard	Kirkop
End Sept	St Francis	Rabat
Early Dec	Immaculate Conception	Cospicua

Health

Malta is a healthy island with standards of hygiene that are comparable to those of Europe and North America. Food is prepared and packaged properly, all tap water is chlorinated (although you can always purchase bottled water) and all milk pasteurised. There is little chance of being struck down by any other type of disease either and no inoculations or vaccinations are needed before visiting the island.

The one thing that can, and does, cause problems is the sun. Malta can be a feociously hot island, particularly during July and August and excessive, unprotected sunbathing can lead to all sorts of medical difficulties that can quite easily ruin a holiday: sunstroke, dehydration, tummy upsets, migraines and 'prickly heat', to name but a few. To avoid these problems is thankfully, quite easy. Firstly, wear a hat; secondly, apply liberal amounts of sun cream (do not mess around with factors two and three: get something that properly protects, such as factor fifteen. You will still tan); thirdly, drink as many fluids as your stomach can handle, even if you do not feel thirsty; and fourthly, sunbathe only for short, fifteen-minute periods at a time, especially in the beginning. Those following these rules will save themselves a lot of unnecessary pain.

Malta has signed reciprocal health agreements with several countries, including the UK and Australia. This means that visitors from these nations can receive free medical treatment in Malta provided that their stay is of less than thirty days duration. This is not to say that separate, private medical insurance is therefore rendered unnecessary and visitors should always purchase appropriate cover before leaving their home country. Any bank or travel agent will be able to advise on a policy that is suitable, although the best type of policy is one that will fly you home in an emergency. Those intending to indulge in any of the activities that insurance companies may consider 'dangerous' — scuba diving and waterskiing for example — should ensure that their policy covers them accordingly.

Visitors who need to bring certain medicines into Malta, or who may need to purchase a specific type of medicine or drug while on the island, would be well advised to come armed with a doctor's letter of introduction.

For minor complaints, visit a chemist. Every town has a chemist, usually open Mondays to Saturdays between 8.30am and 1.30pm and 3pm to 7pm. On Sundays, only one chemist per district will be open. This system is operated on a basis of a rota. To find out which chemist is open on any given Sunday, one needs to consult the Sunday newspaper or alternatively, call the police headquarters in Floriana ☎ 224002.

Most hotels have a doctor on call. Otherwise, in the event of an accident or an emergency ☎ 196 in Malta or 556851 in Gozo. The two main hospitals on the archipelago are:

St Luke's Hospital   **Craig Hospital**
Gwardamangia (near Msida)   Victoria
Malta   Gozo
☎ 241251/247860/234101   ☎ 556851

Language

Malta has two official languages, Malti and English. The Maltese tend to speak Malti at home and amongst themselves but prefer to use English as the nation's business language. Accordingly, most islanders are proficient in both. Yet although one does not really need to learn any Malti as such, a grasp of the basics of the language can come in useful in all sorts of ways, and not least in impressing one's hosts.

Given the hotch-potch history of Malta, it is hardly suprising that Malti is a conglomeration of the various languages of those nations that have, at some time or another, held sway on the island. Its roots lie in ancient Phoenician, hence the semitic nature of the tongue and the fact that vocally, it bears a strong resemblance to Hebrew, Amharic (Ethiopian) and most notably, Arabic. As other nations and their (literally, in the case of the Knights) *langues* arrived on the island, more of their words were incorporated into the islanders own language, as was the script of the later, European occupiers. The consequence of this is that Malti is the only semitic language in the world that is written in Latin script. By way of illustration of the influence of the debt Malti owes to other languages, take these following phrases:

Hello/Goodbye: in Malti this is *saha*, not too dissimilar from the Arabic *salaam* or even the Hebrew *shalom*.

Thank you: *grazzi*, which is clearly Italian in origin.

Good morning/Good evening: *bongu* (pronounced 'bonju') and *bonswa* (pronounced as read), virtually identical to the French *bonjour* and *bon soir*.

Where some knowledge of Malti can really come in useful though, is in identifying the names of towns and villages that are pronounced differently to the way they are spelt. For example, Mdina is not pronounced 'muh-dena') as one would anticipate: instead, one says 'eem-deena'. Expect blank looks if you tell a taxi driver you want to go to 'Hagar Qim': say 'hajar eem', however, and he will take you straight there. Therefore, to help visitors come to terms with the Maltese tongue, there follows here the (29 letter) Maltese alphabet, together the correct pronunciation of each letter.

a (a)

b (b)

c (pronounced hard, as in count)

the 'dotted' c ('ch' as in church)

d (d)

e (e)

f (f)

g (hard as in give)

the 'dotted' g (pronounced as a hard j, like jape)

gh (silent)

h (also silent, except at the end of words)

i (i)

j (becomes a 'y')

k (k)

l (l)

m (normal, except at the beginning of a word when it becomes 'eem')

n (n)

o (as in orange)

p (p)

q (a glottal stop when at the beginning of a word. For example, Qormi becomes 'ormee'. At the end of a word, it is pronounced 'k' as in 'kilt')

r (r)

s (s)

t (t)
u (pronouced as in chute)
v (v)
w (w)
x (becomes 'sh', like ship)

y (there is no 'y' in Malti)
z (hard, as in zig-zag)
the 'dotted' z (soft, as in zeal-ous)

It is really not that difficult. Practice on place names such as Naxxar ('Nash-ar'), Xlendi ('Shlen-dee'), Marsamxett (Marsam-shett) and Mnajdra (Eem-nay-dra).

Mail

Malta's main Post Office is housed in the *auberge* of Italy, Merchants Street, Valletta and is open 8am-6.30pm Monday to Saturday between 1 October and 15 June. Between 16 June and 30 September, the hours are altered slightly, opening and closing 30 minutes earlier, at 7.30am and 6pm. All mail sent *poste restante* to Malta should be addressed to this office.

Sub-Post Offices can be found in most major towns and villages in Malta and, with the exception of the Luqa airport branch, are open during the following hours: 8am-1pm and 4-6pm Monday to Friday. 8am-1pm Saturday. Luqa airport only: 7.30am-7pm Monday to Saturday.

The safest way to send parcels abroad from Malta is via the Expedited Mail Service (EMS) Datapost system. All items sent Datapost from Malta are insured at no extra cost to the postee for sums up to LM 1500, which is a good incentive for the post office not to lose them. The service is expensive and is offered only to those countries with guaranteed delivery times — UK, the USA, Australia for example. Otherwise, one can send send parcels either air mail, surface mail or even Surface Air Lifted, the latter of which is a combination of the previous two. Surface Air parcels (to the UK, USA, Canada and Australia only) are flown out in batches to their country of destination but upon arrival in that country, are then treated as surface mailed parcels. The cost is less than half the price of the air mail service but is, of course, slightly slower.

Maps

A recommended map to use while touring Malta is the AA Macmillan *Malta and Gozo Traveller's Map* scale 1:50,000. This includes detailed town plans of Valletta, Sliema, Mdina, Rabat and Victoria, and a map of St Paul's Bay area, including Bugibba.

For further information contact the local tourist offices on the island who will be more than willing to supply you with maps of the area.

Media

Of the three daily newspapers published in Malta only one is in English, *The Times of Malta* (the other two are *L-Orizzont* and *In-Nazzjon*). Every visitor to Malta should at least buy one copy of this while on the island: so much can be gleaned about a country from a quick reading of a national newspaper. Its football coverage is pretty good too, with special attention paid to the English and Italian leagues, and there is all sorts of other information, such as what films are showing that day and at what cinemas. For a local Sunday newspaper in English, read *The Sunday Times*.

Shops and kiosks in Valletta, Sliema and the other major tourist towns all stock previous-day editions of the most popular European and American newspapers, from the *International Herald Tribune* to *The Sun*. Copies of *Time*, *Newsweek* and *The Economist* are also freely available.

Malta can boast a host of radio stations, some broadcasting in English, some in Malti, and many in both. Island Sound (101.8 FM) is particularly popular, with its standard blend of pop, chat and news although an unusual station worth tuning in to is the Voice of the Mediterranean, a joint Libyan-Maltese venture that concentrates on social, political, economic and cultural affairs and which provides an alternative viewpoint to that obtained in Western Europe. The station broadcasts daily although its hours on the air are limited to 6am-8pm (1557 KHz on the Medium Wave, 9765 KHz Short Wave) and 2-4pm (11925 KHz, Short Wave). The BBC World Service can be picked up on various frequencies on both the Short and Medium Wave bands. The quality of reception, however, can vary greatly: as a general rule, lower frequencies are better early in the mornings and late at night, while higher frequencies are better during the day.

Malta has but one television station, appropriately called Television Malta (TVM) which broadcasts from 8am to midnight. Nevertheless, the Maltese do have access to over a dozen other channels, most of them Italian, which accounts in large part for the fact that so many of the islanders speak good Italian.

Passports, Visas and Duty Free

Citizens of Great Britain (and any other EC member state), the USA, Australia, New Zealand and Canada can enter Malta simply on production of both a valid passport and a return ticket (fixed or open). British Visitors Passports are perfectly acceptable. The visitor is entitled to a stay of up to three months from date of entry but those wishing to stay beyond this time should apply to the Immigration Police, Police Headquarters, Floriana (☎ 224002/220451), shortly before the three months are up.

The following items may be brought into Malta, duty free: 200 cigarettes or 250 grammes of tobacco; one litre of spirits; one litre of wine; perfume or toilet water up to the value of LM 12; gifts up to the value of LM 12. Unlimited amounts of foreign currency can be brought into Malta but only up to LM 50 of Maltese money: up to LM 25 can be taken out out of the country.

Public Holidays

Public holidays in Malta are plentiful and fall on the following days:
1 January: New Years Day
10 February: St Paul's Shipwreck Day
19 March: the Feast of St Joseph
31 March: Freedom Day
Dependent on timing of Easter: Good Friday
1 May: Workers Day
29 June: Feast of St Peter and St Paul
15 August: Feast of the Assumption
8 September: Feast of Our Lady of Victories

21 September: Independence Day
8 December: Feast of the Immaculate Conception
13 December: Republic Day
25 December: Christmas Day

On these days, expect all shops and many museums to be closed. Bars and restaurants, however, will be open as will selected chemists. To change money, go to the foreign exchange bureau at Luqa airport.

Shopping

Shop opening hours vary, but as a general guide most beginning trading at 9am, close at lunchtime for a lengthy *siesta*, and re-open around 4pm before finally shutting the door in the early evening. Most shops, except for the ubiquitous newspaper, cigarettes and fast food kiosks, are closed on Sundays.

Many Maltese souvenirs are of the handicrafts variety and popular buys for visitors include:

Ceramics: an ancient art on Malta, judging by the numerous shards of prehistoric pottery that have been unearthed on the island. You can still buy Maltese pots today, as well as tiles, drink coasters, mugs and so on.

Filigree: this is a very Maltese craft, the art of weaving fine threads of silver or gold into delicately patterned items of jewellery, such as rings and brooches.

Glassware: Maltese glassware is of a particularly high standard, Mdina and Gozo being the best known centres for the art. If it can be blown out of glass, it can be bought on Malta and souvenirs range from vases to decorative fruits.

Knitting: the women of Gozo have acquired a reputation for their knitting and heavy jumpers, shawls and scarves can be seen for sale almost everywhere in the archipelago.

Lace: almost every street market in Malta and Gozo has a stall selling traditional lace work, which can trace its origins as an island craft back to the seventeenth century.

Weaving: another very traditional craft, which has its roots in Roman times when the Maltese were renowned for being fine weavers of sailcloth. You can not buy handwoven sails today but bags, toys, tablecloths, etc are freely available.

For an overview of Maltese handicrafts, visit the Malta Government Crafts Centre in St John's Square, Valletta (opposite the Co-Cathedral), open: Monday to Friday from 9am-12.30pm and 3-5pm from 1 October to 15 June and from 9am-1.30am from 16 June to 30 September.

A warning needs to be issued to those intending to leave their souvenir shopping to the very last minute: ie, on departure, at Luqa airport's small duty free shopping complex. This is the most expensive shopping area of its type that the author has ever encountered. Duty free many of the items there may be, but profit free they most definitely are not.

Sports and Recreation

Clay Pigeon Shooting
Shoots are held on Sunday mornings by the Shooting Federation of Malta and anyone wishing to join them can either write to the Secretary at PO Box 340, Valletta, or ☎ 444747 or 445566.

Football
This is the national sport. The season in Malta lasts from September through to May, with matches played at the stadiums at Marsa and at Ta Qali, on the road to Mdina from Valletta. For news on matches, consult either the local press or contact the island's Football Association at 280 St Paul's Street, Valletta (☎ 222697).

Golf
Marsa Sports Club has a well-maintained eighteen-hole golf course with a professionals shop and the facility to hire out clubs. The course, incidentally a par 68, is open all week, all year round (except Christmas Day and Good Friday) but those hoping for an afternoon of smacking the prune around would be well advised to telephone beforehand (☎ 603809) to ensure that there are no club competitions taking place on that day. Non-handicappers are not permitted onto the course unless accompanied by a handicap certificate player and approved by the professional. Caddies are not available. For more information on the details of the course itself, and on current green fees, contact the nearest Malta tourist office for the relevant brochure.

Horse Racing

A day at the races can be enjoyed on Sundays between the months of October and May at the Marsa Sports Club. Meetings usually feature eight races, most of them of the trotting variety. For more information contact The Race Track ☎ 224800.

Racket Sports

Both Marsa Sports Club ☎ 603809 or 603464 and the Union Club in Sliema ☎ 332011 have squash and tennis courts. The Lawn Tennis Association of Malta, PO Box 50, Sliema, will have information on others. To swat a shuttlecock about, contact the Badminton Association of Malta, PO Box 599, Valletta (☎ 491545) as to the nearest facilities.

Ten Pin Bowling

There are ten-pin bowling alleys at St George's Bay, St Julian's (☎ 341191) and at Enrico Mizzi Street, Msida (☎ 332323)

Walking

The archipelago is ideal for walkers; being so small, nowhere is far from anywhere else and there are usually villages or hamlets en route where one can stop for refreshment. Nevertheless, it is always advisable to take a few bottles of water on any walk, particularly in the summer, in order to avoid the dangers of dehydration. Gozo, green and hilly, is perhaps better for hiking than Malta: despite being smaller than the main island, there is a far greater sense of space and openness. On both islands though be careful if you encounter an 'RTO' sign. This means riservato and signifies that hunters have shooting rights in the vicinity. Accidents are rare but they can happen.

Water Sports

Those who enjoy water sports, from simple splashing to scuba diving, will enjoy Malta. The surrounding seas are warm and clear and pleasantly free of pollution and although sandy beaches are not particularly abundant, there are plenty of rocky ones, the most popular of which are Sliema's and St Paul's. For the best sandy beaches, one must head for either Ghajn Tuffieha, Golden Bay, Mellieha, Cirkewwa or Marsaxlokk on Malta, or Marsalforn and Ramla Bay on Gozo. Comino has two small strips of sand, both privately owned by the island's hotels. Undercurrents are not particularly frequent or strong off the archipelago but as always, one should be wary of them. Every popular beach will have facilities on hand for a whole host of water sports, from water skiing to paragliding, from fishing to windsurfing, and from hiring a rowing boat to going on a 'sausage ride', when passengers are required to clamber aboard what appears to be a giant inflatable pencil (or sausage) which is then towed at furious speeds around the bay. On the subject of speed, one can also hire speedboats, although only upon the payment of a hefty deposit.

What Malta is most renowned for, however, is scuba diving. One can dive off the Maltese coast all year round, each season having its own advantages. In summer visibility will be very good, up to 30m (98ft) while in the winter there may well be more to view, as the fish swim inshore to waters that are warmer and shallower. Divers of all levels of proficiency are catered for, including beginners — there are several diving schools on the island — and equipment can be easily hired.

For those wishing to learn to dive, only a medical certificate is needed in order to prove that they are fit to do so. Experienced divers however, are required to hold a C-Card, a diving permit. This can be obtained for a small fee from the Department of Health upon production of a medical certificate, two passport-size photographs and the diver's logbook. Any diver wanting to dive independently of the island's diving schools will have to present to the same department a diving certificate that is the equivalent of at least the CMAS 2-star certificate. Note that spearfishing is absolutely prohibited.

The coasts of Malta, Gozo and Comino are full of caves and grottoes that in turn, are full of all manner of wonderful marine life, including amberjack, bream, moray eels, octopus, squid and groupers, which are the biggest fish divers are likely to see. Dolphins are rare but then again, so are sharks and causes for concern are limited only to scorpion fish, weaver fish, bristle worm and sting rays.

To learn more about diving in Malta, contact the Maltese tourist office in your home country. When in Malta, useful addresses are as follows:

Federation of Underwater Activities in Malta (FUAM)
PO Box 29
Gzira

Association of Professional Diving Schools
Msida Court
61/2 Msida Sea Front
Msida

Ministry of Maritime Affairs	**Department of Health**
House of the Four Winds	Merchants Street
Valletta	Valletta
☎ 621570	☎ 224071

Yachting

With relatively cheap winter berthing costs, and the construction of excellent small craft facilities at Ta'Xbiex and more recently, at Msida, Malta is fast becoming the yachting centre of the western Mediterranean. The season falls between April and November, and is the time of year when various regattas and races are held, including the Comino regatta in June, the Malta-Syracuse race in July and the Rimini to Malta and back again race in August. For more information on events, and on the possibilities of chartering a yacht, contact the Valletta Yacht Club on Manoel Island, ☎ 331131.

For further information on sports in Malta, and for a brochure outlining the services of Sportsman's Travel, a company that specialises in tailor-made sporting holidays on the island for groups, contact your nearest Malta tourist office.

Telephones

International Direct Dialing (IDD) facilities from Malta are available from any good hotel. Otherwise, employ the services of the Telemalta Corporation which has offices at the following locations that are open at the following times:

St Julian's
Mercury House
St George's Road
Open: 24 hours a day, 7 days a week.

Valletta
28b South Street
Open: Monday to Saturday 8am-6.30pm.

Sliema
Bisazza Street
Open: 7 days a week, 8am-11pm.

Luqa Airport
Departure Lounge
Open: 7am-midnight, 7 days a week.

St Paul's Bay
33 St Paul's Street
Open: 7 days a week,
8.30am-11pm.

Qawra
Triq il-Fliegu
Open: 7 days a week,
8.30am-11pm.

Gozo
Republic Street
Victoria
Open: 7 days a week 8am-
9pm (8pm on Sundays.)

If dialling abroad from any of the above locations, it makes sense to purchase a telephone card (telecard) rather than be fumbling around with coins. These come in units of 60 and 100 and can be purchased at any Telemalta office.

There are no regional codes within the island — just dial the six figure number. Note that Malta is one hour ahead of Greenwich Mean Time, two hours in the summer.

Codes from Malta
UK 44
USA and Canada 0101

Emergency Numbers
Crime and Fire 199
Traffic Accidents 191
Ambulance 196
Police Headquarters, Floriana: 224002/220451/246494
Lost Property 224002/220451
In Gozo dial 562040-2 (police), and 556851 (ambulance)

Telegrams, Telex and Fax
One can send international telegrams, telexes and faxes from the Telemalta Corporation offices listed above, with the exception of the Qawra and St Paul's branches. There are various rates for telegrams, the most expensive being the Urgent Telegram which receives priority transmission over other telegrams and which consequently, is twice the price of an Ordinary Telegram. Cheapest is the Greetings Letter Telegram, which is limited to eleven words only and which must consist solely of either greetings or family news. The Telemalta offices also offer a radio telegram service for contacting ships at sea.

Tourist Offices

Travel

GETTING TO MALTA

By Air

Air Malta operates a daily scheduled flight from London Heathrow and a twice-weekly service from London Gatwick, flying time approximately three hours and fifteen minutes. Prices tend to vary according to season and seat availability, but as a general rule, tickets on these scheduled flights are more expensive than those offered by Air Malta's charter service. These charter flights operate out of all major and a good many minor British airports and can be booked through any travel agent. Inevitably, prices are at their peak during July and August but outside of these months, shopping around can unearth some extraordinary bargains, particularly if one is prepared to leave at a few days notice. All flights to Malta land at Luqa airport where car hire services, money changing facilities and a restaurant/bar are open 24 hours a day.

At present, there are no direct flight connections between Malta and the USA although this may soon change. There is also talk of introducing a long-haul service to Australia, via Bangkok. Check with the Maltese tourist office in your home country as to the current state of affairs.

By Sea
The fastest sea route into Malta is by catamaran from Sicily.
The service is operated by Virtu Rapid Ferries, with vessels
departing from either Pozzallo (journey time 90 minutes),
Licata (90 minutes) or Catania (two hours). The service
operates all year round although departures are less frequent
between October and May. Children under four years travel
free, and those under twelve years for half-price. In addition
to the quoted fare, all passengers must pay a port tax. For
more information, contact Virtu Rapid Ferries at one of the
following addresses:

Malta	**UK**
Ta'Xbiex	Multi tours
3 Princess Elizabeth Terrace	21 Sussex Street
☎ 318854-6	London SW1V 4RR

In Sicily, call either Catania ☎ (95) 384855, Pozzallo ☎ (932)
957245 or Licata ☎ (922) 775955. On normal passenger ferries,
the crossing time from Sicily is roughly eight hours depending on sea conditions. The Gozo Channel Company operates
one such service, between Malta and Catania that runs weekly
between April and June and twice-weekly July to September.
The ferry has space for cars. Further information can be obtained from either Multitours in the UK (see above) or direct
from the Gozo Channel Company at Hay Wharf, Sa Maison,
Malta ☎ 243964-6.

An Italian company, Tirrenia, runs several car ferries to
Malta, weekly from Naples and thrice-weekly from Sicily
(Syracuse, Catania and Reggio Calabria). More details can be
had from either:

Italy
Tirrenia Di Navigazione SPA
Rione Sirignano 2/80 121
Napoli
☎ 720111

UK	**Malta**
Serena Holidays	S Mifsud & Sons Ltd
40 Kenway Road	311 Republic Street
London SW5 0RA	Valletta
☎ (071) 370 6293	☎ 232211

Buses

Travelling on buses is part of the Malta experience and provide the cheapest and possibly most enjoyable way of getting around the island. Almost every town and village on the island is accessible by bus, all services (apart from a few exceptions in the summer season) originating at the island's main terminus which is just outside Valletta's city gate (☎ 225916). Due to the size of Malta, no journey anywhere is particularly long — about sixty minutes is the longest anyone will spend in a seat.

The bus system is easy to figure out. Buses are light green in colour and bear above the windscreen both their destination and service number. Bus stops are easy to identify, looking the same as bus stops do anywhere else in Europe. If in doubt, head for the main square of the town or village you happen to be in, as that is where the stop is most likely to be. As to which bus goes where, look for the notices posted at the open air terminus in Valletta. All buses are one-man operated and passengers pay as they enter; there is no need to tender the exact fare as drivers have change. All buses are non-smoking.

Those intending to regularly use the buses would be well advised to invest a modest sum in a *Malta Bus Map*, published by the Public Transport Authority and available from tourist offices, hotels, the Valletta terminus and souvenir shops. This gives full details of all routes served, including bus numbers, a timetable and fares, which range from the inexpensive to the extremely inexpensive. Note, however, that prices go up some 20 per cent on Sundays and public holidays. Approximate journey times from Valletta bus station to the more popular destinations are as follows:

Senglea (15 minutes)
Vittoriosa terminus (15 minutes)
Marsascala (30 minutes)
Lija, Attard and Balzan, the 'three villages' (20 minutes)
Mellieha (45 minutes)
Sliema (15 minutes)
Cirkewwa (55 minutes)
Rabat (40 minutes)

Gozo's buses are light grey in colour and run far less frequently than those on Malta. All services originate in Victoria. Bus services from Victoria to the port of Mgarr are timed to coincide with the departure and arrival of the ferry from Malta.

The bus service between Luqa airport and Valletta operates every thirty minutes between 6am and 10pm daily, buses from the airport leaving from just outside the departure lounge. However, those intent on using this service to connect with a departing flight should first check to ensure that these times have not since been altered.

Driving and Car Hire

Driving in Malta is in theory quite easy, particularly for visitors from Britain. Driving is on the left, vehicles give way to traffic approaching from the right and there are lots of sensible little laws of the road: a moderate speed limit, for example, of 25mph (40kph) in urban areas and 40mph (64kph) outside towns. All very straightforward, one may assume. Nose a car out into the traffic however, and you may find yourself wondering what exactly has gone wrong.

It is not that the Maltese drive dangerously, or even at reckless speeds. It is just that they drive very badly. So, as to aid the foreign driver in Malta, here are some local 'do's' and 'do nots': *Do not* expect drivers to use their indicators (their cars may not have them anyway) but *do* expect to be overtaken on the inside. *Do not* assume that vehicles will give way to the right at roundabouts but *do* be prepared for vehicles behind you to be crawling all over your rear bumper. *Do not* even assume that drivers will actually drive on the left: the Maltese claim that they like to 'drive in the shade' which is perhaps a little too close to the truth for comfort. Try not to be put off though despite the disadvantages there is no better way of seeing Malta than hiring a car and having the freedom to go wherever you want, whenever.

Car hire rates are among the lowest in Europe and although fuel tends to be expensive, you do not tend to use much. To hire a car one must produce a full, valid national or international driving licence and, in many cases, be over the age of 25 although a number of firms will hire cars to those over 21 who have held a full licence for at least one year.

Local car hire firms tend to be cheaper than the more established, world-wide names but the local cars on offer can be rather delapidated. The local car hire firms are plentiful and advertise their services everywhere, thus making them easy to find. The household names in car hire all have several outlets island-wide (and all have a branch at Luqa airport). Their head offices in Malta are located as follows:

Avis
50 Msida Seafront
Msida
☎ 246640/225986-8

Hertz
United Garage Ltd
United House
66 Gzira Road
Gzira
☎ 314635-7

Budget Rent A Car
Mexico Buildings
Zimelli Street
Marsa ☎ 247111/231077/241571

In the event of an accident, stay with the vehicle until the police arrive as Malta's insurance companies hesitate to pay out unless a police report card has been submitted.

As well as hiring out cars, many firms hire out motorbikes and mopeds too. The same rules apply here, although companies may be more flexible with the 'over-25' law. Crash helmets must be worn and can be hired as an additional item.

Neither a *Carnet de Passage* or a *Triptique* is required by those bringing their own vehicle to the island. A good deal of unnecessary aggravation can be avoided, however, if motorists are in possession of a Green Card, which is an international certificate of insurance that provides third party cover. This Green Card must bear the letter 'M' to show that it is valid for Malta, and must cover a minimum period of fifteen days from the date of entry to the country. Cars whose drivers do not possess a Green Card must remain at the port until a local insurance policy has been purchased. Drivers must also declare that they will not dispose of the car while on the island, unless they are prepared to pay an import duty. The Malta Green Card Bureau is at:
15 Santa Lucia Street
Valletta
☎ 232640

Taxis

As Malta's taxis come in a variety of colours and are often as beat-up and rusted as any other vehicle on the road, they are not always easy to identify. To do so, look at the license plate: if it is red with black numbers, then it is a taxi. All taxis are fitted with meters (most drivers *do* use them) and prices are set by the Government. Wembley Motors, based on the Promenade at Sliema (☎ 311522/332074) operate a radio-controlled, around-the-clock mini-cab service.

By Ferry and Boat

From the beginning of June to the end of October, the Gozo Channel Company operates an almost continual roll-on roll-off ferry service between Cirkewwa in north-east Malta and Mgarr in Gozo, with never more than two hours in between boats. The crossing takes roughly thirty minutes. The service is much reduced during the winter months, dropping to only nine crossings a day. Buses from Valletta to Cirkewwa are timed to coincide with the departure of the ferry, as they are from Victoria to Mgarr in Gozo. The same company also operates another roll-on roll-off service to Gozo, this one leaving from the small Sa Maison port in Pieta Creek, although there is only one crossing daily, leaving at 9.30am and returning from Mgarr at 5.30pm, journey time approximately eighty minutes. During the summer months only, Sliema and Marsalforn (Gozo) are also linked by boat.

The quickest sea route to Gozo though, is by hovermarine, which shimmers across the waters from Pieta Creek to Mgarr in less than thirty minutes. A similar service is offered from Sliema and Bugibba. Prices are more than twice that of those charged on the regular ferry.

Boats serving Comino are operated by the islands two hotels and run only in summer, when there are seven crossings a day to Gozo and eight to Cirkewwa. The larger ferries provide a service in winter (and often in the summer, too) although to no set timetable.

The head office of the Gozo Channel Company is at:

Hay Wharf

Sa Maison

☎ 243964-6

The company also has offices at Cirkewwa (☎ 580435-6) and

Mgarr (☎ 556114/556743). For the Comino-Cirkewwa-Mgarr boat schedule, call Comino hotels on ☎ 473464 or 473051.

Helicopter
Malta Aircharter operates twelve flights a day between Luqa Airport and the Xewkija Heliport on Gozo at a cost which is not quite as expensive as one may imagine. For the regular scheduled flights, note that: an open return is the most expensive ticket; that a day return is slightly cheaper; a one-way ticket is cheaper still; children up to 12 years old travel for half-price and that infants under the age of two pay only 10 per cent of the adult price.

The same company also offers sight-seeing helicopter tours of Malta and Gozo. These operate daily, except for Tuesdays between the months of July, August and September only (although this may soon change) and are of either twenty or forty minute duration. Useful addresses are:

Malta Aircharter
Luqa Airport
☎ 882920-5 (reservations)

Malta Aircharter
Gozo Heliport
Xewkija
☎ 557905/561301 (reservations)

Local Tour Operators
A whole variety of tour operators offer day and half-day trips around Malta and Gozo. Some operators, however, are distinctly better than others, and some employ decidedly dubious tactics. For example, some advertise tours to Gozo that are slightly cheaper than other tours and thereby attract customers. Only when they get to Cirkewwa though, and the ferry boat, do these customers discover that the cost of their ferry ticket has not been included in this price and that they have to purchase this themselves (consequently having to queue for a long time in the sun while ticket holders sit in the shade) which then brings the overall cost up to that of the other, often more established, tour operators. Make sure that the tour guides used by any particular travel agencies are licensed by the Ministry of Tourism as official guides (if in doubt, ask to see proof of this) and ensure that the cost of the tour covers expenses such as the ferry fare to Gozo. Some of the more popular tours include:

An all-day cruise around all the Maltese islands.

A day trip to Gozo.

An historical tour of Senglea, Vittoriosa and Cospicua (the 'three cities').

Comino and the Blue Lagoon.

An historical tour of Valletta.

Mellieha, St Paul's Bay and the *Popeye* village Sweethaven.

A tour of the harbours.

Mdina and Rabat.

The biggest of Malta's tour operators is Captain Morgan's, who offer tours to all of the above as well as some appeallingly off-beat excursions: jeep safaris of Malta and Gozo, for example, which bump over dirt tracks to the more hidden parts of the islands, and vintage bus tours, made in (thankfully re-conditioned) buses that were first used in the 1920's. The company even advertises underwater tours of Malta, in what is said to be the world's deepest diving tourist submarine. For more information, call Captain Morgan Cruises on ☎ 343373 (7 lines).

Karozzini and Dghajjes

Karozzini, heavily be-plumed horses towing flamboyant, canopied carriages are a common sight on the streets of Valletta and Rabat. Use them but avoid any unpleasant misunderstandings, firmly agree a price with the driver before agreeing to a ride: you may want to try your skills at some hard haggling!

Dghajjes, small water-taxis that traditionally make the crossing from Valletta to Senglea, are not as common as they once were. Nevertheless, they can still be found, most notably at Kalkara but also at the Customs House in Valletta or at the Senglea waterside, where a few still serve their old purpose of ferrying passengers across Grand Harbour. Takers however, can be few and those interested should be prepared to have to charter the whole boat. This is, of course, cheaper if you are travelling as part of a group. Those in Malta on 8 September each year should head for Grand Harbour, when *dghajjes* from the suburbs compete in colourful and furiously competitive races.

INDEX